Inspur-r-rational Stories
FOR
CAT LOVERS

by
Niki Anderson

Honor Books
Tulsa, Oklahoma

Inspur-r-rational Stories for Cat Lovers
ISBN 1-56292-618-7
Copyright © 1999 by Niki Anderson
P.O. Box 30222
Spokane, Washington 99223-3003

Published by Honor Books
P.O. Box 55388
Tulsa, Oklahoma 74155

Design by Lorinda Gray and Ragamuffin.

Dedication

To my husband, Bob,
the most dependable person in my life,

to my brother, Michael,
my incomparable "brair,"

and to my cheerleaders,
Goldie Anderson
and
Gertrude Schmehl.

Acknowledgments

I am grateful to Ruth McHaney Danner for her keen critique,
to Christine Harder Tangvald, my long-time mentor,
to Cristine Bolley, my representative and advisor,
to dozens who shared their cat stories, gave me leads,
or granted permission for borrowed material.

I am thankful for my orange tabbies, Earl, Murray, and Myles,
who lay between my keyboard and the monitor
or rolled on my office rug in approval of my progress,
whose devoted presence, never allowed me to tire of my subject.

My final thanks is due the staff at Honor Books who continue
publishing quality works and who believe
cats are on the list of worthy topics!

Table of Contents

Introduction

Cats are primo pets! Just ask any cat owner in one out of every five households in America. There are more than 64 million cats in the United States alone and many millions more around the world. If the 240,000,000 cats who populate the earth were placed nose to tail, that would equal 144,000 miles of cats—a distance more than halfway to the moon. With that many cats meowing and shedding all around us, no wonder authors keep writing about them!

Inspur-r-rational Stories for Cat Lovers is a book for people of all pur-r-rsuasions. Whether cats intrigue you or not, every story offers the reader a truth to apply. People have asked, "Why did you choose cats as a vehicle for teaching life lessons?" I have discovered that humankind learns best through what is familiar. The response to my first book, *What My Cat Has Taught Me About Life,* was gratifying. Letters repeatedly confirmed that not only I, but thousands of others see parallels between cats and life. And, the lessons never cease. Thus, a second collection of cat stories was a natural sequel.

True stories for this collection were gathered from around the world— New Zealand, Norway, England, and Australia; and in the United States, from places as widespread as California, New York, Montana, and Georgia. You will read about encounters between cats and rats, a cat and an owl, a cat and a grizzly, and a touching account about a cat who saved a quail. There are stories about lost cats who were found, traveling cats, rescued cats, over-achieving work cats and underachieving pampered cats, a motorcycling cat,

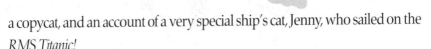

a copycat, and an account of a very special ship's cat, Jenny, who sailed on the *RMS Titanic!*

How each of us lives is based upon the type of stage we select to enact the drama of our lives. There are platforms of intelligence, education, psychology, altruism, and others. This book is written from the platform that God's way is the best way. It is about viewing life with a balanced blend of intelligence, education, appropriate self-interest, and God's eternal wisdom. Reinforcing the theme of each story is also a line of pur-r-rty profound wisdom called the "The Tail End."

The purpose of this book is both to entertain and to inspire. So, settle back and begin to read. You'll laugh, weep, and sigh as you read story after story about the inspur-r-rational felines that grace our lives.

The Saving Grace of Foresight

*M*illions of Britishers hailed a female tabby named Faith during the Battle of London. At the outbreak of World War II, Faith lived in the rectory of St. Augustine's Church, sleeping in her basket on the top floor. Late one night during a bombing raid upon London, Faith gave birth to a single black and white kitten, christened Panda by the rector. With each blast of the exploding bombs, the concerned and protective mother wrapped her paws around her newborn.

One week later, the rector noticed Faith pacing through the rectory as if she were looking for something. At last, Faith returned to her top floor apartment, grasped Panda by the scruff of the neck and toted the kitten to the basement. In a storage cubbyhole, the two prepared for the destruction that would soon strike.

Only three days later, on September 9, 1940, the rectory received a direct hit from a bomb. Faith and Panda huddled in their basement hideaway as the walls collapsed. A fiery explosion reduced the rectory to smoldering rubble. Fortunately, the clergyman escaped without injury.

The following morning the rector remembered the cats and began searching through the ashy remains. His heart leaped when he heard a faint mew. After removing debris, he discovered Faith and Panda in the recessed hole. Though smudged with soot and dust, they were unharmed!

The story of the insightful mother made the front page in London newspapers and brought a bright moment to millions of readers who themselves were under the nightly siege of bombs.

A silver medal was presented to Faith and a certificate acknowledging her "steadfast courage in the Battle of London." Today the certificate and her picture hang in St. Augustine's Church as a tribute to the kitty whose foresight saved both herself and her offspring.[1]

Preparation for good and bad things alike readies us for both survival and celebration. Planning for the future gives us the tools to cope with whatever life brings and appropriate responses for times of celebration. Forethought joined with action is a primary means God uses to prepare us. No action is so futile as preparing too late.

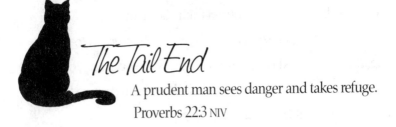

The Tail End

A prudent man sees danger and takes refuge.
Proverbs 22:3 NIV

Mouse Hockey

$\mathcal{A}$lan slammed the garage door and leaned against it with eyes fixed.

"What's wrong, Alan? You look like you just faced death!" Every night Alan stepped out the door to their attached garage to set the burglar alarm. It was as routine as fetching the newspaper off the front porch.

Alan's reply was firm. "Don't go in there. I'll take care of it later."

"C'mon, what is it?" Theresa's curiosity was unquenchable.

It was obvious to Alan that trying to act nonchalant would never convince Theresa to ignore the garage. He might as well tell his wife.

"It's an all-white cat. And no! We can't keep it." The last time Theresa rescued a cat, intending to find it a home, the black and white kitten found a home in the same house with Alan. Sylvester became theirs when Alan met with Theresa's weepy appeal. "I just can't give him up!"

Strangely, Alan had not experienced his childhood allergy reactions during Sylvester's stay. A year passed and he remained immune to Sylvester's dander. Though Alan had grown to love the cat, he still suspected one day he would wake up wheezing, weeping, and sneezing. And now, the thought of yet another feline in the house would add to the risk.

"We've got three Chihuahuas, two parrots, and a love bird. No more cats!"

"Okay, just let me see the cat. We won't let it inside." Theresa shoved him toward the garage. They opened the door and looked into a pair of extraordinary blue eyes. As Theresa lifted the lightweight female, the cat's milk squeezed onto her arm.

"Alan, she's lactating. She must be pregnant. I'll get her some water and food. I'm sure she'll go home." The starving cat gobbled the food like a dog.

Suddenly it dawned on Theresa. "What if she's already had her kittens?" The best solution was to nourish the scrawny cat but allow her freedom to leave. Theresa lined a box with towels and left the temporary bed on their patio. But the cat remained for the next five days.

"Just what we need! Another cat, and an ugly one at that," said Alan. "I knew it, Theresa, that cat isn't gonna leave." Something had to be done. A feline leukemia check was the first necessity.

Theresa made plans to take the cat to the vet after work the next day. But when she returned home Blue Eyes was no where to be found. Theresa called her and within several minutes she heard crying. Theresa spotted her on the other side of their fence, limping.

"Alan, get a ladder," she ordered. At this point, Theresa's complete concern for the cat overruled all sympathy for Alan's imagined allergies.

Blue Eyes tested negative for leukemia and Theresa paid three hundred dollars for the exam, vaccinations, ear mite medication, and treatment for the injured leg. Alan was nonplused. He blamed it all on burglars! If there were no thieves, he would not have needed an alarm system, would not have gone to the garage, would not have discovered the cat, at least not while

Theresa was watching! Drat those criminals! Little did he know he would later have the time of his life playing hockey with this cat.

After bathing Blue Eyes, they discovered a beautiful Dilute Cream Calico with white paws and belly and rabbit length fur. Later, she matured out of her narrow face and fattened into a prize-winning cat.

One night Theresa woke at two in the morning and saw a mouse asleep on the parrot cage in the kitchen. The next morning she noticed more bird seed gone than her parrot would have eaten. This incident repeated itself, until Theresa and Alan could predict every night a mouse would be situated on the cage. After a couple of chases they learned the mice were entering and fleeing under the dishwasher.

"We need an exterminator." Alan was adamant. "This has gotta stop."

"No, that's ridiculous. We have two cats. Besides, an exterminator will kill the mice." Theresa might well have been named Alberta Schweitzer. She loathed killing anything, even bugs.

Alan and Theresa devised a humane plan and set the bedside alarm for 2:00 A.M. When they awoke, the mouse was asleep on the bird cage. Theresa grabbed Sylvester and Blue Eyes, Alan turned his flashlight on the startled mouse, and together they corralled it on the kitchen floor. Alan preempted the mouse by blocking the entrance under the dishwasher with a broom while Theresa shooed the mouse toward the cats with a long handled dust pan, all the while, yipping and hollering.

"Over there, Alan!"

"Get it, Blue Eyes!"

"Eeek!" Get away from me!"

"Good girl, Blue Eyes!"

13

Back and forth Alan and Theresa shuffled the mouse like a hockey puck, scooting it across the slick kitchen floor, always aiming toward the cats. With Alan's left hand, he followed the mouse with the flashlight beam.

The first night's fracas was a failure, but the cats thought the excitement was great. It was obvious that Sylvester would be a spectator in this sport. Blue Eyes was the star player.

The second night their effort was successful. Blue Eyes pinned the mouse; Alan made her give it up and then carried it to a prepared bucket outdoors. Theresa had readied the depository with food and water for the fortunate mouse! The next day they drove to a hillside five miles away and freed the captive. Over the next weeks they caught and relocated at least twenty mice.

When the rodent population was finally eliminated, Blue Eyes continued waking Alan and Theresa at two o'clock. Days passed before she realized hockey season was over.

It was a fair game for all. Theresa and Alan got rid of the mice. The cats enjoyed live entertainment, and the mice lived to teach their offspring the sport of hockey.

It was a fair exchange, as well. Alan and Theresa gave Blue Eyes a loving home, and Blue Eyes gave back by helping dismiss the freeloading mice. Everything that falls into our laps has pur-r-rpose. Blue Eyes was a God-send. When we invest ourselves in whom and what God sends, our investment will always give a commensurate return.

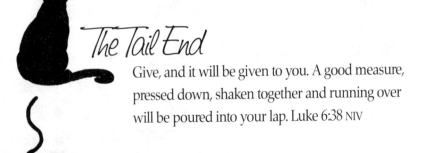

The Tail End

Give, and it will be given to you. A good measure, pressed down, shaken together and running over will be poured into your lap. Luke 6:38 NIV

Impairments That Enhance

A beautiful, long-haired cat struggled for several days to free a hind leg locked in a steel jaw trap. Enduring starvation and freezing temperatures, the blue-eyed captive finally broke through the wire anchoring the trap. Frostbitten, weak, and seriously injured, he dragged himself and the trap to Durston Road in Bozeman, Montana, where he was discovered and rescued.

Humane Society workers welcomed the mutilated survivor. They began with eyedropper feedings and veterinarian care. His right rear leg required amputation, later earning him the name Stubby.

Frostbite also took a large toll on Stubby's body. He lost part of a paw, the tops of his ears, the toes of his left leg, and four inches of his apricot-tipped tail.

What Stubby did not lose was his affectionate nature. His owners, Carol and Bill, describe Stubby as king of the castle. Stubby is also a spa cat—he likes showers, though he objects to towel drying. He relishes aggressive brushing and allows anyone to pet him. When Carol returns from work, Stubby follows her with meows and reaches out with his paw to invite a

stroke on the back. His handicaps have not disabled his love for people. "You can't resist a cat that pulls himself over on three legs and sits at your feet," says Carol.

Stubby's physical impairments have only enhanced his personality. His expressions of love require more effort than those from cats unchallenged with physical handicaps. Stubby may have three legs instead of four, but his contributions of affection are fourfold those of some cats. The family believes they are fortunate owning a cat who demonstrates every day that impairments can bring enrichment.

Wholeness can best be measured by a people's disposition rather than their composition. Malformed bodies may have suffered the disfigurement of disease, trauma, or genetics. When physically challenged people adopt an attitude like Stubby's, the result is enhancement, not detriment. Attitude blemishes are a flaw. Physical impediments are only a condition.

The Tail End

Life offers no damage insurance claws.

Hurry Home

*T*he McHaney family was enjoying their last days of respite at their summer cottage in the upper peninsula of Michigan before heading home to Arkansas. Everyone was busy packing and completing tasks necessary to secure the house until their return the next year. Sneaking a break, Linda meandered outdoors to enjoy the lessening rays of summer sunshine and to breathe the fresh air wafting from nearby Lake Superior.

In view was an open field where her cat Fifi and dog Missy liked to roam. Linda's attention was suddenly drawn toward the grassy field by a piercing wail from a cat in distress. Then there was silence. Linda gave little thought to the distant noise as her eyes were pulled upward to a sight she would later recall. An owl was lifting his winged body into the sky clutching something unidentifiable. Like pieces of a puzzle that do not immediately connect, Linda failed to associate the cat cry with the owl in flight.

Later that afternoon she missed Fifi and began calling, "Kitty, kitty, Fifi, come home!" Fifi was seldom gone more than a couple hours. Even Missy,

the collie mix, seemed disturbed by Fifi's absence. By evening the rest of the family had joined in the search.

Linda's mother assured her that Fifi would likely be home by morning. That evening Linda put Missy on the covered porch for the night without her feline companion. The practice of putting the pets to bed was intended to protect them from wildlife in the area. Bears, coyotes, and other country creatures were a threat to beloved pets.

Linda awoke the next morning with the sad reminder that Fifi was gone. "Mom! Is Fifi home?" Linda ran to the back door, but no black and white kitty greeted her. Tomorrow they would leave. The thousand-mile drive to Arkansas demanded that they depart as scheduled. Linda's heart ached as she blinked away tears. Fifi *had* to come home that day.

The hunt became more intense. Throughout final preparations to leave, each family member aided the search. Linda's father drove to the neighbors to ask about Fifi, everyone took turns calling her, and whenever someone was found in an unusual place or position, the explanation was simple–"I just thought I'd see if Fifi was there."

At daylight that third morning, Mr. McHaney roused the family to load the car. He drained the pipes, Mrs. McHaney made lunch for the road, and Linda cried. "We can't leave without Fifi," she begged. Her mother let her keep the litter box in the car until ten minutes before they left. Sparing Linda, at last Mrs. McHaney dumped the box of litter into the rose bed.

The moments were somber as the last suitcases and boxes were squeezed into the car. Linda's crying had regressed to the agony of quiet sobs. "Fifi!" Linda kept calling between pauses to blow her nose.

A neighbor dropped by to bid the McHaneys farewell. After hearing about Fifi he commented, "Could've been an owl. I've seen 'em carry off rabbits." By then Linda had completely forgotten her recent sighting of the owl.

At the bleakest moment before Mr. McHaney called everyone to the car, Linda thought she heard a faint "meow." She insisted on one last investigation. As she ran toward the cry, she spotted the tail of a cat. From the tall grass emerged Fifi, as relieved and as happy to see the family as they were to see her. "Fifi! Fifi!" Linda screamed with joy. She ran and scooped up the cat and buried her face in its fur, dampening it with her tears. Mom cried too, Dad beamed, and Linda's older sister Ruth pleaded, "Let me cuddle her!" Even Missy ran to lick Fifi and wagged her tail to signal her delight.

"I guess you'd better shovel the cat litter back into the box and load it in the car," Mrs. McHaney told Linda. Linda gripped Fifi under her arm as she quickly scooped the litter, now dotted with fallen rose petals, back into the cardboard box.

At last it dawned on Linda. "I know what happened to Fifi! An owl did carry her off. I heard a cat's cry and then I saw an owl fly off with something. It was Fifi. I wonder how she got away?" Ruth and Linda examined the cat and discovered patches of missing fur, some scratches and nicks, but no serious wounds. It was not unlikely that Fifi had escaped from her captor and then headed home—a distance only Fifi knew.

The drive back to Arkansas was a pampered journey for Fifi. Linda fed her tidbits and held the cherished cat on her lap most of the way.

The day that Fifi encountered the hungry owl, her adventure in the field went a-fowl. Like the stealthy descent of an owl upon an unsuspecting cat, life sometimes sweeps us away with terrifying surprises. If we are fortunate enough to escape with our bodies and emotions intact, like Fifi, we are wise to point ourselves home where the welcome, aid, and consolation of family, friends, and neighbors await.

The Tail End

Dear God, help me move beyond the shock of life's calamities and seek help from the family, church, and community that waits to support me. Amen.

Celebrate the Celebrity

For Heather, Christmas was more than a season to anticipate a new catnip mouse. The black and white kitty taught everyone in the Simons' household the most important lesson of Christmas.

The year Mrs. Simons purchased a crèche, she and her children situated each figure as Heather watched nearby. Young Jolene suspected the cat would be curious. "Heather looks pretty interested, Mom." But Heather waited for a later hour to do her sacred investigation of the new Christmas attraction.

The crèche was complete as Jolene laid a tiny facsimile of an infant in the barn-style bassinet. The miniature holy family and the attending shepherds stood beside the manger in poses of adoration.

The next morning the children ran to the tree to plug in the lights. Someone stopped to admire the crèche and called, "Mom, baby Jesus is missing!" A thorough search of the house revealed the culprit was Heather, who had enjoyed her own silent night with the Christ child. Jolene snatched the figure from the reluctant cat and returned it to the manger.

The following morning, Heather was found again with baby Jesus nestled between her paws. Once again Jolene returned the infant to the straw bed. By the third morning the family knew Heather would *not* be found chewing on curling ribbon adorning the Christmas presents. Neither would she be batting at tree ornaments or following the smell of baking fruit cake into the kitchen. Heather was focused on only one thing—the Babe in the manger. She lay near the crèche with the figure of Christ tucked under her neck.

As Mrs. Simons looked on with the children, she seized the opportunity to teach them the lesson that Heather was demonstrating. "It looks like Heather is focused on the real meaning of Christmas. Not the tinsel, not the traditions," she said. "Maybe we all need to place more emphasis on the Gift of God's Son, the true Celebrity of the holiday." The Simons' children liked the suggestion that Heather was setting a good example. Heather had established the prominence of the Christ Child for every Christmas thereafter.

The festivities intended to celebrate a person can easily distract from the person being commemorated. Candy canes and poinsettias can be misdirected focal points at Christmastime. Tropical orchids carried by a bride should not detract from her beauty any more than Christmas tree lights should outshine the Light of the world.

The Tail End

Put the em-paw-sis in the right place.

A Better Way

*B*ailey and Marble have lived together for eight years, happily disproving the assumption that dogs and cats are enemies. Bailey, a male poodle, and Marble, a calico shorthair, are a loving duo. Bailey whines at the basement door if Marble is shut downstairs, and Marble grooms Bailey's curly leg with sisterly devotion. When Bailey returns from his daily walk with owner Lisa, Marble welcomes Bailey at the door with an arched caress.

A famous literary pair, known as "the gingham dog and the calico cat," did not enjoy such a happy affiliation. 'Twas half past twelve and neither the gingham dog nor the calico cat had slept a wink. Situated eye to eye on a table top, they endured one another with growing hostility. Suddenly the checked dog and the colorful cat announced their mutual annoyance with a loud "Bow-wow," and a reply of "Me-ow!" A Dutch clock and a Chinese plate watched with dismay as shreds of gingham and tufts of calico littered the air for the duration of an hour. Teeth and claws, bites and scratches, snarls and spits, created a midnight drama unpleasant to behold.

Next morning where the two had sat
They found no trace of dog or cat;
And some folks think unto this day
That burglars stole that pair away!
But the truth about the cat and pup
Is this: they ate each other up!

This poetic account by Eugene Field describes a dog and a cat in regrettable contrast to the amiable poodle Bailey, and Marble, his affectionate calico colleague.

Fighting consumes the contenders and ends in the annihilation of peace and dignity. When people duel with words, sometimes the outcome is costlier than dueling with swords. Fighting can be a worse adversary than even an enemy. Bailey and Marble illustrate how it is far more pleasant to "love up" one another than to "eat up" one another.

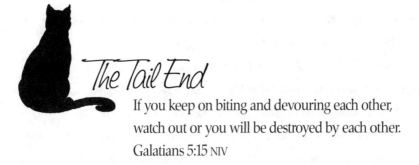

The Tail End

If you keep on biting and devouring each other,
watch out or you will be destroyed by each other.
Galatians 5:15 NIV

Better Together Than Alone

On Sunday morning, May 18, 1980, Alice and Paul Schneider hurriedly dressed. The drive to church was a thirty-minute trip, and they still needed to call their cats indoors. Alice noticed Kit, Boots, and Eeney through the large picture window of their new mobile home. "Look at those three, Paul." The cats sat shoulder to shoulder, as if posed, each facing Mt. St. Helen, northeast only twenty miles. The Schneiders lived on five acres of wooded land about two miles from Randle, Washington.

Alice called the cats from the front door. They ran inside but were restless and garrulous. Alice talked back. "Kit, what's all the worry?" The cats paced the house and kept gazing up, tails erect, bodies alert.

Suddenly a blast sounded that was heard for hundreds of miles around. The Schneiders instantly connected the wariness of the cats with the source of the noise. At 8:32 A.M. the sleeping volcano of the Washington Cascades had erupted, blowing away thirteen hundred feet of the mountaintop. The cats' keen senses must have felt the subterranean activity. Boiling mud, hot

ash, deadly gases, and steam billowed nine miles high. A wake of destruction included eight deaths, mud slides, floods, ravaged bridges, buried automobiles, and lightning storms that ignited forest fires.

Many residents on the mountainside had evacuated earlier when geological readings indicated turbulent conditions inside the volcano, but the Schneiders were not within the evacuation radius.

"After the explosion we weren't even frightened," Alice said, "but we began thinking ahead quickly. Paul drew water from the faucet and filled containers. He hauled inside a store of extra wood for the stove." The cats, who normally scooted between legs and darted outside at the turn of a door knob, were content to settle in. Instinctively they chose shelter indoors.

Within ten minutes a rain of ash turned the bright spring morning into a black and eerie night. A flashlight held to the window revealed a dark fog. Having canceled their church plans, Alice and Paul conducted private Sunday worship beside the wood stove as they clasped hands and thanked God for one another. Three cats blinked their amen. In the midst of the cataclysmic event, their togetherness brought strength and calm.

The next day, a neighbor drove through the blanket of ash to bring them face masks. He warned them that people *and* pets were huddling under cover for hundreds of miles around, until scientific analysis of the ash could be completed and reports issued. Kit, Boots, and Eeney remained inside for two more days.

By five o'clock that evening power was restored, and the last sprinkle of ash fell to the ground. Paul slipped on his mask and began shoveling out. An ash barrier eight inches deep made it impossible to open the back door. He managed to push open the front door and cleared the deck of ash that weighed 90 pounds per cubic foot.

On the third day after the explosion, the cats took their first cautious steps outdoors. Each time they returned, Alice popped them in the bathtub. Black sooty paw prints were not welcome on the new carpets. Kit's cream-colored coat was soiled to a taupe shade that did not become her. Boots' white paws changed to gray.

As wind, rain, and time slowly cleansed the earth, the cats and the Schneiders returned to life as normal. They were among the many who lived to share the story of a volcano's eruption. That historic Sunday morning began with traditional plans to attend worship. But the passages in life involve both routines and disasters. The Schneiders and their cats proved that life's eruptions are weathered best with others beside us.

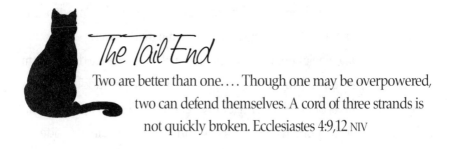

The Tail End

Two are better than one.... Though one may be overpowered, two can defend themselves. A cord of three strands is not quickly broken. Ecclesiastes 4:9,12 NIV

Fire Drill

*L*ights and sirens alerted traffic to the oncoming fire truck as a crew of firefighters responded to what they supposed was a routine call to extinguish a chimney fire.

For the caller, the September evening had begun mildly. With romance in mind, Dana suggested Tim rent a video and build a fire. His favorite meal bubbled in the oven. Dana lit three pink tapers and completed the table setting with cloth napkins. The candlelight supper would set the mood for a cozy date at home.

Tim was in favor of the idea. "What movie shall I get?" he paused at the door.

"Something we both enjoy. Nothing violent, preferably romance or comedy, no war flicks, stars we both like, but *especially* action . . . "

"Whoa! I'll try, Dana, but remember, I'll be renting something I haven't previewed, so I can't be sure of everything. Okay?" Tim wanted a vote of confidence.

Dana was agreeable. "That's fine, honey. I just want to be together with the phone unplugged. I'll grit my teeth through any bad parts."

Tim was back soon. They lingered over dinner and finished with pie a la mode. While Dana rinsed the dishes, Tim headed for the fireplace, arranged kindling, and added a few alder logs. He tossed in a match and stepped back as the fire ignited.

"C'mon Dana, let's start the movie. I've got a nice fire going." But before Tim had a chance to press the remote, the tone of the evening changed abruptly.

A flying spark had set fire to a nest in the chimney. Four inflamed squirrels dropped down the flue and leaped into the living room. Dana screamed. Like little torches on legs, the squirrels began running throughout the house.

Tim snatched a towel and began chasing an emblazoned mother squirrel and her three fiery offspring. Dana replugged the telephone and dialed. "Send a fire truck! Four squirrels are running through our house—on fire—what I mean is, the *squirrels* are on fire!" She shook her head and cupped her mouth with her hands. The mother squirrel sped past her, stopping long enough to drop and roll, a strategy she repeated, then resumed her aimless pursuit.

Missy, their black and white cat, was alarmed by the uproar and looked stunned when a tiny squirrel skirted past her. The odor of smoke cautioned the wise cat. She ran to the underside of a chair and watched the action with widened green eyes. It was the most excitement this indoor cat had witnessed since the painters had moved all the furniture.

Before Tim could corner any of the afflicted creatures, the large squirrel fled to the basement. "Close the door on the squirrel!" Tim yelled, but Dana was distracted.

The first of the baby squirrels had succumbed. "Oh no, Tim, I think it's dead!"

"Quick Dana, close the basement door!" Who knows why Tim thought the basement was a better place for the mother squirrel.

Events escalated rapidly. Missy darted from under the chair and Tim gave another order. "Put Missy in the basement. She'll go after the squirrel!"

The senseless decision destined Missy for certain danger. Mindless of the impending consequences, Dana set Missy on the top step and slammed the door as the fire truck wailed its arrival. "Go after her, Missy!" she called. Dana had also misjudged whether the cat would assault a burning squirrel. Poor Missy must have been bewildered by all of the chaos whirling around her.

The two firefighters stepped into the smoky house and saw three deceased squirrels and heard a lot of commotion in the basement. The growls and howls of a cat defending itself against a frenzied squirrel sent one of the firemen tearing downstairs.

He opened a window to encourage the squirrel's escape, but a little too late for Missy's sake. The mother squirrel had perfected the "drop and roll" technique well enough to quench the fire that singed her fur. She dashed out the window.

The cat was nowhere in sight. Upstairs, a fireman checked the chimney to make sure the fire was out. Now the question was, "Where's Missy?"

The four of them began to search. Huddled in a corner among shoe boxes was the injured and traumatized cat. She was missing whiskers and a chunk of ear-tip, hair was gone from a spot on her head, and her body was scratched by the squirrel's sharp claws. She meowed her confusion as the fireman handed the trembling kitty to Dana.

"Oh, Missy, I'm so sorry, we thought *you'd* have the upper paw." Dana and Tim began to assess what had transpired during the past thirty minutes with less emotion and more rationale.

"I guess that was a bad idea, putting Missy in the basement. What a donnybrook! At least the house didn't catch fire." Tim shook hands with the firemen and thanked them. He promised to take Missy to the vet and get the chimney cleaned before they used the fireplace again.

As Tim closed the door behind the men, he reached his arm toward Dana. "Well honey, you wanted 'lots of action' when you sent me for that movie. Are you satisfied?".

They laughed and hugged.

The conversation between the firemen as they headed back to the station was a little different. "I'd like to know whose been holding survival classes for park squirrels. That mother squirrel is alive only because she kept dropping and rolling. Too bad she hadn't had a chance to teach her offspring."

Missy was a victim of circumstances no one could have foreseen. Under normal conditions, Tim and Dana would never have endangered their beloved cat, nor would Missy have become embattled with an enraged squirrel. Circumstances may leave us feeling thrown to the lions after emotional and uncalculated decisions are made. Sometimes, in spite of incurred losses, the only comfort may be found in the realization that worse outcomes were possible. At times, simply being alive is our greatest consolation.

The Tail End

Surviving the exigencies of life is a noble accomplishment.

Everyone Needs a Wing and a Prayer

Ten acres of dairy farm belonging to the Bjerland family nestled comfortably in a river valley of Kristiansand in southern Norway. Daisies budded, fruit trees gave promise of harvest, and the big chestnut trees would soon ruffle in white blossom. Farm- and pastureland were surrounded by hills of dense timber that in wintertime stoked the wood stove in the 200-year-old farmhouse. The diversified farm was home to horses, pigs, chickens, rabbits, dogs, cats, and twenty-one milking cows.

It was 1943. Roald Tangvald, grandson of the Bjerlands, was just six years old. His parents and grandparents were active in the underground resistance to Nazi occupation. The conflict, which later resulted in the death of several family members, overshadowed the normally idyllic farm life. Amidst the national tensions, smaller tragedies on the farm speckled day-to-day life.

The Bjerlands' cat population included about two dozen cats (including the tomcat from a neighboring farm). "We supplemented the cats' diet of

barn mice with a pint of fresh milk twice a day," said Roald, now an American citizen of over fifty years.

Added to the bevy of cats weaving among workers laden with milk buckets were the hens, running, squawking, and sometimes tumbling a farmer. They tracked under horses, equipment, and boots. The Norwegian egg layers (similar in appearance to American leghorns) were kept in the pens during the summer. In the spring, a few were chosen to breed and were allowed to run freely. The cats were trained to respect the hens and chicks. When a rogue feline chased a chick, the cat was sure to receive a corrective swat on the haunch. But, when adults were not watching, the children also chased the chicks. The angry hens would then turn on the children who broke into laughter as they raced away.

Roald clearly remembers a double mishap that wet and foggy spring. One of the white hens hatched only four chicks, a smaller than average brood. She made her nest where the mowing machines, wagons, and trailers were stored in the barn. Sadly, two of the unnoticed brood were crushed to death when a wagon was pulled from among the equipment.

The following day, misfortune struck again. A large truck arrived to collect the milk spann (bucket) and transport it to a co-op for processing. "That morning the truck lumbered up the road and maneuvered close to the barn," Roald recalls. "Early morning darkness and fog hindered visibility. The truck ran over and killed a mother cat and two of her four kittens. Now there were two kittens without a mother and one hen without two of her chicks."

Young Roald set out to rescue the orphaned felines. He knew the bed of the kittens was in the same section of the barn as the nest of the bereaved hen. He crouched to look before reaching and beheld an empty cat bed. A

soft cluck from the nearby hen drew his gaze toward her nest. Roald bolted for the farmhouse. "Mama! Papa! Come look! The kittens are with the hen and chicks in her nest!" Fur or feather was irrelevant to the motherless kittens. Family and work hands hurried to look and marvel at the mismatched group of downy fowl and furry felines sheltered under the wings of a hen.

Still there was a problem. The hen's adoption would not substitute for milk. The kittens needed to be fed around the clock. Roald's uncle snatched them from under wing several times a day for eye-dropper feedings. Even when he was busy with chores he sopped a cloth with fresh milk and squeezed nourishment into tiny pink mouths. Each time he removed the adoptees from the nest, the incensed hen protested with flapping wings and a determined chase. She was most content when two chicks and two kittens were under wing. Not until the kittens were older did they begin acting like cats. While they needed it the most, they accepted the feathered warmth and the plucky protection of their mother hen.

In all climes and countries, among all ages and races, amidst pain or privation, humankind needs a wing of refuge. The Norwegian kittens sought cover under wings that were nearby. How easy it is to forget there is no closer refuge than the wingspan of God. Divine shelter is as close as a prayer.

The Tail End

The LORD repay your work, and a full reward be given you by the LORD God of Israel, under whose wings you have come for refuge. Ruth 2:12 NKJV

Never Quit Pur-r-raying

*M*ost children come home from a visit to Grandma and Grandpa's with a remote control car, a tale about a carnival trip, or something consumable like a bag of Gummy Bears™. To his parents' dismay, six-year-old Clay returned from a weekend at his grandparents' lake cabin with a treat of a different kind.

Before Clay pulled his duffel bag from his grandpa's car, he called to Pat and Floyd. "Mommy, Daddy, wait 'til you see what *I've* got!" Grandpa avoided eye contact with Clay's parents.

Pat and Floyd stood on the porch with wide smiles. When Clay unloaded a black and white kitty, their grins remained but their eyes communicated a dozen objections, which only Grandpa perceived.

"I named him Tiger like the cat in the storybook, Mommy."

In unison, Floyd and Pat responded. "Oh!" Their reply was brief but their reaction was not so succinct. Floyd could not imagine why his parents, who had never owned one family pet, had allowed this development. Besides, Clay already had calico Elmer (later renamed Elmette, following the birth of her five kittens).

Floyd's mind was racing. Most little boys stuff grasshoppers, frogs, or lizards into their pockets. Not Clay. He had found a stray cat. A frog could be taken to the pond and freed. A lizard could be assigned to insect control in the rock garden. But a cat! A cat is so clingy! A cat solicits the emotions and begs to stay without uttering a meow. A cat demands a decision and the only acceptable decision is, "You are welcome to stay, be fed, bedded, petted, doctored, and (at times) endured (when you are obdurate) for the next fifteen to eighteen years." Unlike Clay, Pat and Floyd knew inviting a cat into their life was no casual decision. But turning away a homeless cat was not a simple decision either. Owning Elmette and her offspring Cottonball had transformed Floyd and Pat into true ailurophiles (cat lovers!).

So Tiger stayed. He was a delightful contrast to melancholy Elmette. If Tiger had been a man, he would have given shoulder massages, called you "dear," and helped with the dishes. Tiger was a lover. As a bonus, his presence seemed to lessen Elmette's mood swings.

Many months later, Tiger left for his morning adventure but did not return by nightfall. Clay was distraught. When he and his mother said bedtime prayers, Tiger was the main topic for God's attention.

"Dear God, you know where Tiger is. Tell him to come home and take care of him. Amen."

Such were the prayers that ascended heavenward for the next few days: "Dear God, I miss Tiger. Please bring him home."

For the following weeks: "Dear God, Tiger must be lost. Lead him home."

Without fail, every night for months to come: "Dear God, feed Tiger until he comes back."

A variety of phrases always expressed Clay's love and persistent faith. When Clay said grace at the dinner table his petition included blessing on both the cauliflower and the missing cat. Even the Sunday School teacher mentioned Clay's prayers for Tiger's return.

One year passed and then another. Pat, knowing the menace of cars and coyotes, still remained as steady in her faith as Clay. One night, as Pat considered her son's faithful petitions, a thought came to her that prompted her to lift her own prayer. "Lord, how are You going to handle my little boy's faith? He's been asking for two years and believes You are going to bring Tiger back." She headed to bed and left her question with God.

The next morning, she looked out the kitchen window. Across the lawn and beyond the empty swimming pool approached a prancing cat. The cat's determined and quick step was an imitation of Elmette when she came seeking commendation for a mouse kill.

Then Pat noticed the kitty was black and white. This was nothing new. She had been comparing black and white cat markings to Tiger's for two years. But this cat came right to the door and acted like he wanted to come in—even expected to be invited. Pat went to the door, cracked it open, and saw he was Tiger! He welcomed her embrace as she scolded him for leaving and kissed him for returning. There was no doubt he was Tiger—he was as distinctly recognizable as a dear friend.

Clay came home from school to discover the best answer of all his childhood prayers. "He was thrilled to see Tiger," Pat told Floyd, "but he took it in stride." It was clear that Clay had been merely waiting but never doubting that Tiger would come home.

The model of faith is the faith of a child. When prayer is offered with childlike trust, God listens and sometimes cats come home.

The Tail End

Pray continually. 1 Thessalonians 5:17 NIV

Mission Impromptu

The Grand Coulee Apartments have been home to hundreds of people in Spokane, Washington. In the historic downtown complex, a college student shares her studio-size living space with Madeline, a black and buff striped cat. Madeline unfailingly rewards Jodie with a fond and peppy reception each night upon her return from long days away at school and work.

Each day, Jodie listens to hours of lectures and seminars and then settles behind her desk in the university's News Room, where she puts in hours more of reporting, copy-editing and layout for the campus newspaper. Second to Jodie's day-end weariness, Madeline is her next best reason for going home.

Maddie-Girl, as Jodie calls her, is polydactyl. Madeline was named after a character in a short story by Ernest Hemingway who owned many six-toed cats. The appending toe on each of Maddie's feet spreads outward like a thumb, giving her paws the appearance of two furry hands. On the petite six-pound cat, whose adult face retains a kitten visage, the large feet are comically unproportionate.

The little cat is a frolicsome handful of affection. In less time than it takes Jodie to unload an armful of textbooks, Maddie has found a toy and laid it at Jodie's feet. The two play fetch until Maddie's lungs heave with deep breaths and her little heart races. Jodie then tucks her under an arm and plops on the bed with her lively companion. Maddie gives Jodie lick-style kisses and walks in figure eights, pausing to give rubs of devotion against Jodie's sleepy head. When Maddie settles down, she curls her soft body on the pillow half that Jodie reserves for her.

Everyone seems to love Madeline—Jodie's friends, parents, and as Jodie later discovered, even a resident in an upstairs unit.

One evening, a girlfriend was visiting Jodie and left the door ajar. Maddie stepped out at eleven o'clock, unnoticed. When Jodie finally realized Maddie was missing, she began searching the hallways, upstairs and down. By two-thirty in the morning, Jodie was frantic. Besides, it was not an appropriate hour to be calling through the corridors, "Maddie, Maddie-Girl, where are you?" The sprightly little cat was not around and Jodie was in tears.

At three in the morning, Jodie made "Lost Cat" signs and posted them on each floor. Her telephone was out of order, so she dialed her boyfriend from the main floor pay phone. She wanted to tell someone who would sympathize. As tears wetted her cheeks, a stranger startled her with a tap on the shoulder. "I think I've got your cat," said a large white-haired man.

"Really?" she exclaimed. She quickly hung up and followed the man who appeared to be in his seventies, though a bit apprehensive about this large stranger leading her to a different wing of the apartment building two floors above.

Jodie looked inside his door before walking in and spotted the confirmation of his story. "Maddie!" Jodie scolded. In one glance, it was plain Maddie was enjoying the novelty of the experience. There she sat, perched on a table with front feet tucked under her chest, as if nothing particularly unusual was going on at that four a.m. moment. "Fixed in her position and watching out the window," said Jodie, "she turned her head toward my voice and looked at me nonchalantly. She chirped a greeting, as if to say, 'Oh, hi Mom!'"

Jodie sighed. Maddie was okay—not wandering downtown streets and alleys, not forever lost.

Apparently, Maddie had been discovered by the gentleman, who introduced himself as Teddy, when the venturesome cat padded to the third floor. It had been a wakeful night for Teddy. He had moved from a smaller apartment and was still unpacking. He too had stepped into the hallway that night and happened onto the curious cat who was exploring the Grand Coulee Apartments.

Teddy had invited Maddie in. "She's a little *too* friendly," he chuckled. Maddie had offered him shin rubs and thoroughly investigated his apartment. He had prepared her a litter box of shredded newspaper, fixed her a soft bed, and fed her ravioli! He was not prepared for a feline visitor. For several hours the pair enjoyed each other's company.

Teddy's apartment was a stark contrast to Jodie's. A smoky haze filled the room. Boxes were stacked in random places, and the decor of the sparsely furnished room matched the age of the elderly cat-sitter.

"As I entered Teddy's world, momentarily I felt guilty, knowing I would leave with my cat," said Jodie. "It was obvious Teddy had enjoyed Maddie's company, and was maybe secretly glad it would be a more suitable time to search for her owner in the morning. I visited with him a few minutes, thanked him and left. The long night of anxiety had drained me," Jodie said.

"Maddie strained under my tight grip as we walked back to my apartment. Her insomnia and my exhaustion were not a good blend. I climbed into bed. Maddie realized her adventure had been curtailed when she took her place on half of the pillow and we both went to sleep."

Sometimes our carefully scheduled agendas expand to include unplanned ministries that are more important than the duties we jotted on our lists. So it was with Maddie. She set out to tour the apartments but ended up entertaining a lonely old man. Maddie never finished her tour; though agendas are important, so can be the detours.

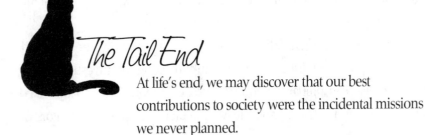

The Tail End

At life's end, we may discover that our best contributions to society were the incidental missions we never planned.

Hector, the Protector

"*B*elieve me, there is a rat in my house!" Rose shuddered. Just saying the word *rat* incited repugnance and deepened her concern. She hung up the telephone suspecting her landlord doubted her. She could imagine his reaction. Did he suppose she was simply a single parent with two small children and a big imagination?

Rose and the children had lived in the rental house for only a few weeks. Around eight o'clock every night, Rose heard noises that began behind her kitchen wall and traveled toward her pantry. Other hints of an intruder were nibble punctures on sacks and boxes of food. She could not find a hole to plug so she began sealing her staples in plastic containers. The thought of vermin in her house created a fear as foreboding as the rodent itself.

Throughout the days before calling her landlord, she could only surmise what was dwelling within her walls. Her wildest supposition was a trapped boa constrictor escaped from a previous renter. Or maybe it was a family of mice. Her neighbor suspected a water rat from the nearby drainage ditch that ran between their houses. This speculation proved to be correct.

One evening the rat made a brazen appearance—pink tail trailing behind his quick legs. Rose gasped as the rat shuffled under her kitchen table. "Every fact and fantasy about rats flashed through my mind," she said. "I ushered my children upstairs and we stayed in our bedrooms for the rest of the evening."

It was time to call the landlord. The night he paid his visit, the rat obligingly showed himself again. The landlord caught a passing glimpse and appeared a bit squeamish himself. "I don't usually allow animals in our rentals, but with a fella' like that roamin' around, I suggest you get a cat."

Rose was working toward her bachelor's degree at Oberlin College and noticed an ad in the campus newsheet. "Free cat. Long-haired neutered male."

Rose packed the kids in the car and drove off to answer the ad. The current owner had inherited her feline tenant the same way Rose had inherited the rat—unwanted. Allergic to cats, the student was anxious to find an adoptive home, but not nearly as eager as Rose was to abolish the rat.

Home they went with high hopes and a nameless pet. "Mommy, what should we name him? Can we call him Fluffy?" Rose was more anxious to turn him loose in the kitchen at eight o'clock than to decide upon a moniker.

Nevertheless, within the week the cat became Hector. Rose had read *The Illiad* a few months earlier and admired Hector, Homer's fearless and valiant warrior. She hoped the namesake would be prophetic of his success in battle against the rat.

Not disappointing his new family, the intrepid cat set out with military fervor routing moles, mice, and the rat. The walls became silent and Rose's

fears were quieted. Hector earned his keep and lived up to his name as valiant protector.

The Hector of literature balanced his courage in battle with kindness and gentleness toward his family. Similarly, the feline Hector demonstrated traits of patience and affection. Rose's four-year-old daughter would drape Hector over her arm like the straps of a purse. Hector lovingly yielded dangling limbs. He often slept at the foot of the children's bed and when Rose sat on the couch, Hector curled up on her shoulder, purring his pleasure. A defender indeed, but a loving defender was Hector. His actions matched his name.

Reputation gives birth to names. Hector's name truly reflected his character. Both good and bad names stick fast. Therefore, live to inspire a good name rather than provoke a bad one.

The Tail End

A good name is more desirable than great riches; to be esteemed is better than silver or gold.
Proverbs 22:1 NIV

The Learning Curve

The drivers were young. It was the 1960's. A blizzard raged. And the cats were the smartest creatures riding in the car.

It never occurred to Melody Peterson and her husband that the cats might have preferred to stay home. A car and gas money were a big deal for college students in those days. Their excitement would be their cats' excitement, they figured. And so it was. Charles and Cybele saw Ohio from the rear seat . . . whoops! the front seat . . . whoops! the dashboard of their old Renault.

Charles, a long, sleek tabby, looked smashing in his red leather harness. Cybele, a fluffy gray and white beauty, sported a light blue one. Into the Renault they piled. Buckle up? There was no such thing back then. With a turn of the key, they were off.

The feline twosome adapted with ease. Start-the-motor time meant bound-from-window-to-window time. Eventually, the cats' outrageous curiosity was followed by an orderly retreat to the back seat where they napped peacefully until the car stopped. Charles and Cybele drew attention

at supermarkets and gas stations. Most people simply were not used to seeing cats appear in car windows.

On an earlier trip during their Thanksgiving break, Melody and her husband had tackled some real mileage with cat passengers. In the process of trekking from Ohio to Pennsylvania, they soon learned that cats will not walk on a leash at designated rest areas, or use a litter box in a moving vehicle, or even use the litter box at a convenient time. Charles and Cybele were more likely to request a stop five minutes after departures from rest stops.

Now in December, the winter put all of them to a much more formidable test as long-distance adventurers. Never mind the blizzard. Or the fact that their Renault burned nearly as much oil as it did gas. Albeit, the heater heated. The windshield wipers wiped. And the gas money supply was . . . almost adequate. In fact, going home to see the folks with their young felines in tow actually seemed like the right thing to do.

The wind howled and snow flew. Safety soon dictated that big rigs find the way while the Renault cautiously followed in their wake. Charles and Cybele slept without a care.

As the blizzard intensified, one endless hour merged into the next. Little by little, the highway emptied of all but the big trucks and the big fools. Then, sometime after midnight, the car went glub-blub-blub. They had a flat tire. Melody and her husband exchanged wary glances. Charles and Cybele pranced around the back seat as Melody's husband rolled into the snowbank at the side of the road.

Were they prepared and optimistic? Of course! They had their cats. They had their youth. They also had a spare tire and one pair of gloves to share. Cold air whistled into the car. The cats bounced to the front seat and nested on Melody's hands while her husband grabbed the gloves and changed the tire.

Several freezing minutes later, they hit the road again. In the wee hours of a wintry dawn, they began to notice rental trailers in ditches, station wagons in snowdrifts, and trucks jackknifed along the sides of the interstate. Fear finally began to grip them. Finances, however, did not permit stops for a motel room or for restaurant meals. Gulping hard and following another trucker, they continued on until … blub-blub-blub … yes, they had another flat. Mr-r-row!

This time Charles and Cybele sang in earnest. As the car limped into a mechanic's bay, sleepy attendants came out to hear the feline "music," croon a few affectionate words of their own, and repair the tire. Everyone seemed energized by the sound of supervisory meows and the sight of bright, round eyes appearing first at the side window, then at the back.

An hour later, they began the homestretch. Gingerly cruising down icy Route 66, they broke into Christmas carols. At every traffic light, the cats sprang up for a look and a comment. Almost there. What a relief. It was fun. "Joy to the World." No more … glub … problems?

Glub-blub … mr-r-rROWWW!

Thirty years later, Melody can appreciate the incredulity of relatives who watched them arrive seven hours late with two cats, one pair of gloves, and a clunky car listing badly on its third, dead-flat tire.

"Today, we would never travel with cats unrestrained. In our mature wisdom, we avoid marginal cars, insufficient travel funds, and weather that hints of anything less than bliss. We've also learned the presence of pets can lower human blood pressure. How fortunate we were that '60's winter.

Charles and Cybele provided companionship and entertainment. They also did their part in calming the course of a very hazardous escapade."[2]

The learning curve is often a treacherously winding road. Since most of us arrive at adulthood, we can suppose God provides extra mercies as we navigate the highways and byways of youth. Like Melody, her husband, and their naive cats, when we are young adults, we set out with little regard for possible hazards. Like them, we usually escape unscathed. But impulsive decisions may lead us into cat-astrophes that in the later wisdom of adulthood we would thoughtfully avoid. Thank goodness God's mercies extend to cats and He joins us on our journey along the learning curve to maturity.

The Tail End

I trust in the mercy of God forever and ever.
Psalm 52:8 KJV

Medic Cat

"*S*haron, wake up!" His voice anxious, Sharon's husband shook her shoulder. "There's been a coup attempt! The road is blocked; I can't get to work." It was December 3, 1989, at the beginning of a bloody uprising in the Philippine Islands.

Sharon tensed with fear. She had dreaded getting caught in the midst of government unrest when Gary accepted the overseas job in Makita, Manila. Now she was faced with her worst imaginings. Callers from the embassy warned them not to step outside. For the next five days they remained prisoners in their downtown apartment while gunfire cracked and bazookas boomed. Trying to cope with the panic provoked stomach upset and headaches.

"After three days of listening to artillery, I could tell the difference between a 30-caliber and a 50-caliber machine gun," said Sharon. The view from their picture window added to the horror of the conflict. They could see puffs of smoke ascending near President Aquino's residence. Worse yet,

parked in front of their apartment building was an armored transport vehicle whose driver sat motionless, shot and deceased.

When the shooting escalated on the final night of the siege, they made their bed on the floor of a windowless hallway. One living room window had already been shattered. After the cease-fire, they would discover bullet holes in the back porch.

Those five days of terror destroyed Sharon's emotional health. She began to experience severe depression, daily headaches, and nights of insomnia. Memories of the gunfire and violence left Sharon edgy, jumpy, and unable to concentrate on any task long enough to complete it. After a visit to the doctor she was diagnosed as having post-traumatic stress disorder.

Sharon sought the company of others, which was not typical for a lover of solitude. "I turned to friends and music, read the Bible, and prayed regularly. I was still tense and nervous all the time. I found myself praying constantly, 'Please God, help me to feel like myself again.' How could I have guessed the means God would send to answer my prayer?"

A short time later, Sharon and Gary moved to Malaysia where he took a position with an electronics firm in the capital city of Kuala Lumpur. As Sharon prepared for the move she resolved to do two things to soften the transition and treat her emotional instability. She would buy a piano after they settled (she had neglected the piano for twenty-five years) and she would also get a cat (she hadn't had one since childhood).

Once in Malaysia they began house hunting and found a nice bungalow with a bonus. The previous renters were looking for a home for their blue-eyed part-Siamese cat, named Nusu. Sharon was delighted with the package deal—house and cat. They took them both. Gary was reluctant about having a cat, but he agreed under the stipulation that she was Sharon's responsibility.

Nusu began her healing ministry the first day. "I loved her instantly," said Sharon. "Nusu was now with me as I continued to battle recurring feelings of anxiety and depression. Though I no longer felt the threat of political upheaval, loneliness engulfed my spirit. Gary had work colleagues, but I knew no one in the large city. Nusu became a tangible support."

In the weeks that followed, Nusu was Sharon's closest companion. She always stayed nearby. "If I typed a letter, Nusu lay on the desk and napped. If I read, she cuddled beside me. When I ate, she'd follow me to the kitchen and I'd serve her a treat, so we could dine together. When I returned from outings, she'd meet me at the door with a meow. I'd whisk her up and whisper in her delicate ear, 'You're such a blessing to me, Nusu.'" Within a couple months Sharon realized she no longer felt the smothering loneliness.

However, she was still plagued by nightmares of violence, flashbacks to the coup attempt. She would awaken fearful and agitated and then feel Nusu's rough tongue licking her face. When she lay back down, Nusu snuggled beside her. "Listening to her soft purr lulled me to sleep," she said. With Nusu "the medic cat," Sharon's emotional healing continued and nightmares were fewer.

Nusu also revived Sharon's joy and laughter by providing lively playtimes. She would chase Nusu who ran in circles throughout the house. Nusu would stop suddenly, poke her ahead around a hiding place, and look at Sharon convinced she was unseen. "Nusu, where is Nusu?" Sharon would call. "There she is!" With gleeful blue eyes, Nusu would dart out and the game would start again.

Nusu also brought a touch of healing to Gary and Sharon's marriage. The strain of the coup and a major geographical move created an emotional distance between them. Nusu won Gary's heart by preferring *his* lap over Sharon's. After he got acquainted with Nusu's sweet nature, he admitted one night, "I guess she's not such a bad little cat." Their mutual enjoyment of Nusu gave them something new to share.

Sharon credits Nusu for nursing her back to emotional strength. "The recommendations of my doctor, the kindness shown by new friends, and the ministry of music through my piano helped restore my emotions. But Nusu's constant presence was the best medicine of all. I thank God often for the calm she brought to my life."

Sometimes God bottles His prescriptions in fur.

The Tail End

"When God wrote the inviolable law that requires living things to need one another, He included the entire animal world." Pets offer "the kind of responses needed to increase our emotional reserves." [3]
Dr. Richard A. Swenson, M.D.

The Conduct Factor

*V*ivian Cristol, writer and past magazine editor, adopted Charlie, an orange stray roaming the streets of Greenwich Village in the 1960's. Among Charlie's many aberrant characteristics was his aversion to handling. He objected to being carried about, or even picked up briefly. Vivian surmised that onlookers must have wondered whether the cat was unmanageable or the owner was incompetent. Either way, the impression given was negative. In fact, Charlie and Vivian lost a chance at fame and fortune for this very reason.

A casting call had gone out from a Hollywood studio for the supporting role of a cat for Audrey Hepburn in the forthcoming movie, *Breakfast at Tiffany's*. Having read the book, Vivian recalled the description of the cat: a large male tiger cat, orange, New York apartment-type (Charlie was *all* of that), not too elegant or svelte (absolutely Charlie), and preferably a bit weathered by the outside world (once again, Charlie!).

"I didn't think of Charlie's vagaries at all," Vivian later recalled, "only his good points and how right he was for the part." She popped him into a

carrier and taxied up to the Commodore Hotel, where some fortunate feline was about to be discovered, perhaps Charlie.

Hundreds of people crowded several large public rooms of the hotel. Black cats, white cats, Siamese and Persian, dainty females and belligerent males, most of them obviously spoiled and all of them present against their better judgment. Long lines led into the judging room with a rectangular table covered in green felt. Four emissaries from the movie company stood beneath glaring spotlights, matter-of-factly noting the parade of hopefuls.

As the owners waited, they filled out forms and compared statistics and stories about their cats, while the animals themselves hissed, arched, and glared at one another, plainly unhappy with the whole event. Charlie, like the rest, was agitated, but Vivian's mind was sidetracked with dreams of her future.

"I could see myself ensconced in one of those directors' chairs somewhere near the set, knitting perhaps, and observing with quiet pride as my son, the actor, sat on Audrey's lap kneading with his claws some stunning Givenchy creation she would be wearing." As Vivian dreamed of a glamorous life, it never occurred to her that during the audition Charlie would be lifted—yes lifted, handled, held—taken from his carrier, placed under hot bright spotlights, and exposed to four studious strangers.

When Vivian and Charlie neared the head of the line, the facts of the audition overturned her daydreams. Butterflies began flitting about in her stomach. "Has there ever lived a cat with less savoir faire than Charlie?" she asked herself. Suddenly Vivian was second-guessing the whole wild idea. What had possessed her to think she would be able to handle Charlie in a setting like this? Why hadn't she thought of a tranquilizer—for him, of course! In a last-moment attempt at preparation, she talked soothingly to Charlie, opening the carrier lid to accustom him to the lights and people.

"Next," spoke an examiner who summoned them forward with a hand signal.

"I wish I could say Charlie surpassed my wildest expectations and brought the house to its feet in a thunder of applause with his performance. That was not quite the case." Vivian lifted him from the carrier as he struggled every inch of the distance to the table. In a split second he tore loose from her grasp, gripped the green felt with all fours, gathering it into a heap, and almost toppled a pitcher of water before diving under the table. One of the judges groped under the voluminous folds of felt and dragged Charlie out, holding him cautiously toward Vivian, while wearing an expression that was a pitiful mixture of amusement and rejection. Everyone laughed and some even applauded. "That was our one moment of glory," said Vivian.

When the newspapers announced the part for a cat had been cast, Vivian read that the winner had film-making experience. That was the likely explanation with which hundreds of other hopefuls, including Vivian, eased their disappointment. "But what humiliation, to have the whole world know we weren't ready for Tiffany's!" she exclaimed.

The most disappointing result of all was that the cat chosen for the role looked exactly like Charlie. His maladjustment had undoubtedly made the difference between a life with Charlie in Greenwich Village and stardom in Hollywood.

Indeed, personal demeanor can make a difference as wide as the distance between New York and California. The manner in which we

conduct ourselves often determines rejection or selection. As early as grade school, children are judged by their behavior. Later in life, roommates, employers, landlords, and coaches will commend or refuse us on the basis of our attitude and conduct. Remembering to manage ourselves with savoir faire is particularly crucial when the spotlight is upon us. The way we present ourselves is a critical factor in every part of life.[4]

The Tail End

Charity ... doth not behave itself unseemly.
1 Corinthians 13:5 KJV

Nursery Duty

*S*eventeen-year-old Rob Mann has no memory of life without Midnite, his female cat of equal age. One day, when Rob was a mere toddler, the black cat with two white whiskers followed him and his mother, Debbie, home from the bus stop. Day after day Midnite faithfully trailed behind Rob, until finally, on a cold and windy day, Debbie pitied the cat and gave her a bowl of food. When she refused to leave the doorstep Debbie finally let her indoors. Within the hour, Midnite declared herself mistress of the household by napping in the center of Debbie's bed.

Rob was a likely candidate for a cat in need of a good owner. His love of animals was evident even as a young child. At the age of four, he joined the 4-H club, and would continue on to serve as vice-president in his teens. The Berrien County 4-H Extension Office awarded the high school senior a county medal for his achievements in working with animals.

Most valuable to Rob is Midnite's lifelong companionship. "She's a real loving animal—a good old cat," said Rob. "We're pretty close, Midnite and me. She proved it when we moved from St. Joseph to Eau Claire. Midnite was

about twelve years old. To get her used to the new area, we left her in Eau Claire with my grandma for a few days before we moved there. Three days later Grandma called and said Midnite was gone. The Humane Society picked her up in Benton Harbor, only three miles from our home in St. Joseph. She'd traveled twelve miles in her attempt to return to us. She was in good shape, though. We were sure glad to see each other."

After Midnite's adoption by the Manns, she established herself as guardian and caretaker of the young animals who are nurtured at the Mann's five-acre mini-farm in Eau Claire. "She's always got babies to care for," said Rob, "and has always commanded the respect of the animals we've owned."

Rob's 4-H projects often require a newborn animal of various species. Debbie willingly converts her master bathroom into a nursery. Ducklings and baby geese splash in the whirlpool bathtub while Midnite sits on the edge of the tub supervising their first attempts at swimming.

One year Rob raised a turkey for the small animal auction at the fair. He placed the caged turkey in the bathroom under a heat lamp. Midnite tended it for over a month. Whenever it chirped, Midnite looked anxious and led Rob or Debbie to the bathroom. Often, there was a genuine need like replenishment of food. "Midnite would circle the cage and appear relieved that we responded," said Debbie.

One of Midnite's favorite charges was a Nubian goat. Rob put the ten-day-old goat in his bedroom inside a portable dog kennel. During the day, Midnite watched, slept, and groomed beside the cage. The little goat had to be fed around the clock. Midnite maintained a clean environment for him by licking up drops of spilled formula after feedings. Though Midnite seldom goes outside, when the goat wanted out, she followed behind and waited on the front steps until he returned, then followed him back to the kennel.

For several years the Manns had a feisty teacup poodle named Pierre. He got along with no one but Midnite, probably because Midnite made it clear that she was the boss. They became soul mates. Midnite let Pierre sleep with her in the cozy oval cat bed. It was an unlikely sight, the tiny but grown dog sleeping with a cat three times its size.

Midnite's gifts of nurturing and devotion have paid a return in personal acclaim. She has placed in the Berrien County Youth Fair competition for several years, in 1997 as Reserve Champion Cat Overall and as Grand Champion short hair. In 1998 she was awarded Grand Champion Overall. When the nearby town of Cassopolis, Michigan, hosted a two-day event honoring the inventor of cat litter, Midnite reigned over the festival as the female feline sovereign and was recognized with a Lifetime Achievement award as the oldest competitor. But the Manns contend Midnite's most prestigious achievement is her attitude toward all the pets in their home whom she could have viewed as rivals rather than as youngsters in need of her care.

Perhaps Midnite has never forgotten how scary it was when she was a homeless cat. When the Manns adopted her, she was less than a year old and obviously lost. Could it be that she remembers what it was like to be young and to yearn for a caregiver? Maybe that's why she has a heart for all the chicks, ducklings, puppies, and goats she has nannied over the years.

Feeling compassion for those who have endured misfortunes similar to our own is a powerful way to salvage a negative experience. Midnite went a step further. She turned her compassion into kind action by nurturing the young lives of other animals.

The Tail End

Bad experiences are best redeemed when we attempt to spare others from a similar plight.

Painful Waits

$\mathcal{I}$t was time to move. Business opportunities lured Mike and his wife from the rural life they had enjoyed for several years. Their city venture was located only 120 miles away, so they moved in spurts. Mike's cat, Pretty Thing, was left to guard the old house while the new one underwent remodeling. Friends agreed to check daily on Pretty Thing and make sure food and water were available.

The plan seemed acceptable to Mike. But evidently, the arrangement felt like abandonment to his six-pound pretty kitty. The day Mike and his wife arrived to get Pretty Thing and transport the last load, she was nowhere in sight. Mike called and looked, but there was no response. Every armload from house to truck ended with a "kitty-kitty" call. But Pretty Thing did not appear.

P.T., affectionately abbreviated, was as much a part of the family as any of the two-footed members. She had been with Mike through years of life's exigencies, both good and not so good. Mike's spirits sank at the thought of leaving without her. Though the truck was full with possessions, it looked empty without Pretty Thing. Time was running out. Beth Anne, Mike's wife, read the concern in her husband's face.

Moments later, both of them perked to a familiar sound. "Listen, Mike!" said Beth Anne. She recognized the many-meanings-meow of Pretty Thing. "Meow, meow, meow," pause, "meow, meow, meow." But Mike heard something different. His special relationship with Pretty Thing gave him an edge on interpretation. What he heard was, "Wait for *me!* Wait for *me!* Wait for *me!*"

From across the tumbleweed field and down the unpaved road, her cry grew stronger and stronger. And then, there she was, walking swiftly and a bit indignantly. *Why was I left?* her quick steps spoke. She purred and scolded in a contradicting mixture that made Mike smile. With one hand he scooped up his little gray cat and off they went.

Pretty Thing forgave Mike his egregious transgression, and she spent the next eleven years as close to the center of his life and his lap as she could. But time began to slow her down. The routines of life became more and more difficult for her, though she could still make the leap into Mike's always-welcome lap.

The inevitable day came that every pet owner must face. Beth Anne called Mike at work to tell him that Pretty Thing was very near her end. They had watched Pretty Thing digress for a number of months. It was the call Mike had dreaded. But work at his pottery shop detained him. "I told Beth Anne I'd be there as soon as possible," said Mike. "My mental cry to my old friend was an echo of hers from eleven years past at the old house when she had cried out, 'Wait for me! Wait for me! Wait for me!' I wanted to be with her before she slipped away."

Mike worked fast and left the store in charge of helpers. He arrived home to discover that Pretty Thing had waited. She was still alert enough to greet him. "We bid one another farewell," said Mike. "My companion of sixteen years parted from me shortly thereafter. I cried a lot, and still cry when I think about Pretty Thing."

"Wait for me" is an age old request. We utter it at good times when we want to be part of the fun that is about to happen, "Wait for me!" We also speak it at hard times, like Mike, when we know we must take part in a difficult situation. No one likes to wait, but we all hope others will wait for us. The next time we must wait for someone, it may help to remember that someday our turn will come to ask, "Please, wait for me."

The Tail End

Waiting for others validates their worth.

Pick of the Litter

*T*asha purred as she fluffed the fur of her month-old kittens. Five in a row, they nuzzled against her soft belly, yielding to each swipe of their mother's tongue, and listening as she trilled her affection. Tasha's pride was plain to see. She may have secretly suspected that she was reputed for bearing the loveliest Maine Coon cats in the area.

For a cat of unknown bloodlines, and not blessed with beauty herself, Tasha's consistent production of show-class offspring must have amazed even her. She was short-haired with mottled gray, white, and yellow fur. But among her ancestors there undoubtedly had been a Maine Coon philanderer. Her handsome kittens, usually blue-gray or soft yellow, and always long-haired, were in high demand.

Tasha's most recent litter was composed of Smoky, a solid gray kitten; Mittens, a gray kitten with white chest and feet; Buttercup, an all gold feline; and a long-haired calico named Charlotte. Then there was nondescript Hawthorne—specially christened by Tasha's owner Becky.

Perhaps Tasha objected to the name Becky chose for her peculiar kitten, but Hawthorne was unique in more ways than just his uncommon moniker. His coat was short and bristly. The fur was yellow and white, a shade that gave the impression of unintentional sun bleaching. For lack of a more enhancing hue, Becky described his color as dirty beige.

The tricolored male was an anomaly even by sex. Ninety-five percent of calico cats are female. For weeks Tasha licked Hawthorne's neck and right front paw, hoping to erase two dark spots. Tasha may have felt shamed when she concluded at last that the patches were permanent gray fur—and *she* was the mother of a tri-colored tomcat! From then on, Tasha hid Hawthorne under her tail or back paw. He was an odd one among her four other quintessential kittens.

Hawthorne was unlike his siblings in yet another trait. He cared nothing for rolling and tumbling with the others. He preferred attacking the family dog. He had a superior air that earned him Tasha's frequent cuffs about the head and ears.

At mealtime Hawthorne's manners were atrocious. He growled at his fellow diners and tried to push the others out of the nursing basket. Though he started out as the runt of the litter, it was clear he did not intend to stay small. His appetite was gluttonous. Had it not been for Tasha's efforts at curbing his misbehavior, the other kittens may have starved.

When Tasha began weaning the kittens, Becky realized they would soon be ready for new homes. News spread quickly. The phone began ringing with callers interested in Tasha's famous litters.

Imagine Becky's astonishment when the first kitten selected for adoption was the infamous Hawthorne. If cats blush, Tasha was likely pink under her whiskers. A little girl named Jenny chose him because she said she liked his "funny spots." If mother cats wince when their kittens are taken, Tasha may not have felt much pain. Maybe she looked forward to a few trouble-free days with her four remaining beauties before they, too, were adopted.

But Becky had not seen or heard the last of Hawthorne. He turned out to have hidden talents. In fact, one particular gift bought him his ticket back home. The budding actor excelled at sick-and-dying scenes. Just two days after he left, Jenny and her mother brought him back.

"I'm so sorry," said Jenny's mother. "We fed him what you recommended, but he's been deathly ill since the moment we brought him home. He won't eat or play. May we have Buttercup, instead?"

Hawthorne looked limp and spiritless—totally unlike him. But as soon as Jenny and her mother left with Buttercup, Hawthorne revived completely. With the sound of the car droning off in the distance, he leaped from the basket and attacked the dog, sending the surprised terrier howling for protection. Losing Buttercup was hard enough for Becky, but trading Buttercup for Hawthorne was an incredulous twist.

In the following weeks, all of the kittens found homes—all but Hawthorne. Each time someone came to choose a kitten, Hawthorne performed his near-death scene, or jumped on the dog, or hid in the garage until everyone was gone. He intended to stay. He may have presumed someone needed to keep Tasha humble and keep the terrier in his place.

Strangely, after all the kittens were gone, Hawthorne settled down and changed into a perfect pet. He became the darling of Becky's family and the attentive companion of Ralph, the aging terrier. Nonetheless, Tasha would

have nothing to do with Hawthorne. In disgust, she had given up on him long before his mellowing behavior became evident.

Hawthorne led a long and exciting life. He gave up acting and took up fishing when Becky's family moved to a house near a river. He continued his faithful friendship with Ralph, lying with him in the sunshine on the dock, and even sleeping on the same pillow with him at night. It was best for both of them that they died within a short time of one another.

Becky has tried to imagine what it was like at heaven's pearly gates when Ralph and Hawthorne arrived. Though the Bible is silent about the presence of animals in heaven, it isn't very hard to picture an imaginary scene. The doors would have swung open widely for easygoing Ralph, Becky is sure. If Hawthorne had any doubts about himself, the heavenly conversation may have gone something like this:

"Do You have a place for me, God?"

"Why of course, Hawthorne. In my eyes, *everyone* is the pick of the litter."

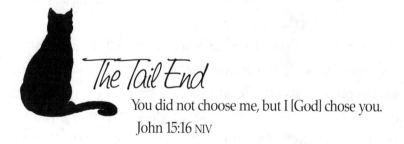

The Tail End

You did not choose me, but I [God] chose you.

John 15:16 NIV

Pur-r-rfect Timing

"Please don't think I'm strange," a woman caller began, "but I keep hearing sounds like a crying child in the sewer system in front of my house. I heard the cries yesterday and again today as I walked past the manhole."

That sultry July evening about ten o'clock, a fire department dispatcher noted the report. His voice then came over a speaker at number eight fire station alerting personnel to respond. The possibility of an endangered child warranted an immediate investigation.

An officer, driver, and firefighter pulled red Engine Eight from the large garage to answer the call. Having arrived at the manhole, Officer Dietrich and Firefighter Baron squatted to listen more closely. Indeed, it was a cry, but not from a child. They recognized the mournful plea of an unhappy cat. The woman caller came from her house to thank the men, in time to hear Dietrich say to Baron, "It's a cat. Right?"

"Pretty sure." It was not the first time the men had heard a similar cry from a trapped cat.

"I sure appreciate you guys coming." The woman sounded sincerely grateful. "I wasn't gonna sleep another night until someone checked this out."

There was water just three feet below the street level. Above the water were adjoining pipes, and from a connecting joint came the pathetic wail.

Officer Dietrich was first to devise a plan for extri-cat-ing the feline. "You two stay here. I'll go across the street," he said, pointing to the other manhole. "We'll try to flush it out with a mild pressure spray of water. Hagle and Baron waited at the opposite end to catch the cat when it exited. It was crucial to grab the distressed animal before it fell into the water.

Dietrich turned on the pump and placed the nozzle of the booster line down in the manhole and into the connecting pipe. The sudden rush of water did more than coax the fear-frozen animal from its dark imprisonment. The cat fled like a fluffy torpedo, meowing and skidding to a stop at the end of the pipe. Baron grabbed the panic-stricken cat, whisked it out of the hole, and lifted it over the street. But Baron lost the struggle to hold the unwieldy animal as it twisted, clawed, and maneuvered out of his hands in a leap toward freedom. They watched the collarless, thin, mangy, gray and striped cat flee to a questionable destination.

For all three of the officers the event was more than an act of duty. Both Hagle and Deitrich were cat owners. Throughout the rest of the shift they theorized about the cat returning home, or the not-so-cheerful possibilities, if the cat was homeless. Would it find food after its unknown length of confinement? As they logged their report in the station journal, they felt satisfied they had done what they could. Shortly after, they realized the full implications for the cat had it remained in the pipe.

An hour and a half passed and a storm rolled over the city with clapping thunder and torrential rains. A gray tabby owes one of its nine lives to the men at station eight and to a sensitive woman who cared enough to call professionals. Had the cat not been freed, it would have drowned in the flooded drain pipes.

As Hagle, Deitrich, and Baron answered calls related to lightning strikes and power outages, they noticed flooded streets everywhere. "Sure is a good thing we got that cat out," was the refrain of the night on the rig. "Sure is a good thing."

And perhaps the woman caller who watched through her front window at the heavy rainfall bouncing on the streets, thought to herself, *Sure is a good thing they got that cat out!*

Yes, it truly is a good thing that God's timing is perfect. If He cares enough to provide for the rescue of a cat just before a big storm, how much more will He order the events in the lives of His children?

The Tail End

My times are in your hands. Psalm 31:15 NIV

Rising Above What Surrounds

James Stephen Behrens boarded a train between Newark and Morristown in New Jersey one morning after rush hour. The almost empty commuter afforded a quiet and private tour as he gazed at the quickly passing scenery.

It then occurred to the trappist monk that trains tend frequently to track through ruinous parts of cities. He watched the quality of the scenery deteriorate. Litter abounded on both sides of the tracks. Strewn bottles and garbage, discarded furniture and shreds of clothing filled the landscape.

The backsides of apartment buildings and houses were also exposed. Back porches were accumulated with scrap. Sagging telephone wires, rusty wrecks of cars, corroded lawn furniture, broken windows, and patched roofs represented the broken lives of residents.

Suddenly the train slowed and then eased to a stop near a bridge. The distant voice of the conductor hinted at an unexpected wait. Spray paint

graffiti colored the dirty cement. An abandoned factory loomed to the left. Tall smokestacks stood with pigeons perched in the crumbling brick work.

Father Behrens then fixed his eyes at sights below his window. A collage of refuse filled his view again. Within the stretch of an arm were pieces of cardboard boxes, a mangled doll, a single sneaker, a shoe heel, a ripped wallet, soiled diapers, and tangled coils of wire.

These symbols of brokenness, unhappiness, struggle, strife, and poverty aroused deep compassion within him. Suddenly his eye caught a movement. From a large pipe emerged a cat who paused, looked about, studied the train, and only then cautiously moved forward. Trailing behind were four frisky kittens. Less leery than their mother, they bounced along, inhaling the scents and investigating each new thing. The mother had advanced about 30 feet from her young, then retraced her steps and returned to check on the kittens. She smelled each one and then chose one to lick from top to bottom—the literal bottom. The kitten received her mother's ministrations with joy. After the final lick, the kitten hurried off to join siblings and redeem every moment of the day.

"I was truly fascinated by all of it," said Father Behrens. "The mother was proud and watchful of her offspring and was oblivious to the human influence in her surroundings."

The train jolted and heaved and then began to move again. The cats passed from view. Father Behrens craned his neck, watching them as best he could until they could no longer be seen from the window. Then he sat back and wondered why it felt so good merely seeing something so ordinary as a cat and her offspring.

After a short time of reflection, Father Behrens realized the profound lesson taught by the mother cat and her kittens. "I concluded that despite the sad and troubled state of our cities, beauty abounds in nature and in the lives of those behind broken windows. Some still dream and love and hope. They strive to rise above their cheerless environment and retain dignity amidst ruin. Amazingly, art, literature, compassion, and courage will be born in these settings. Humankind can learn from the example of a mother cat who can blink at her surroundings and answer the call to the more important demands of every day."

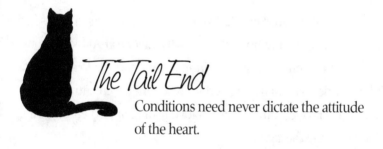

The Tail End

Conditions need never dictate the attitude of the heart.

Room for Flexibility

$\mathcal{S}$andy and her mom loved to fish. Two uncles from past generations had been professional fishermen who trolled the salty waters off Alaskan shores. A grandfather held trophies for prize-winning trout and made sure all his grandchildren participated in fishing derbies when they were growing up. It was natural for everyone in the family to love fishing and to enjoy frying, smoking, and canning the catch.

Betty was visiting her daughter Sandy at their beach-front home on Lake Coeur d'Alene in Idaho. That morning the sun rose over still waters. "C'mon, Mom, grab your hat and pole. Let's go snag some perch for supper." No coaxing was necessary. Betty kicked off her slippers and tied into her sneakers.

The grown women skipped to the dock. They stepped into the bobbing rowboat and paddled a short distance. When they found a peaceful pool, they anchored. For the next two hours they wormed hooks, cast, and sipped coffee from a shared thermos. There were few bites and only one success, but they had no regrets. "Well, Mom, it was fun as usual, one fish or none."

Betty's touchy back had endured its limit on the hard seat of the boat, so they paddled back with one small perch in their bucket.

The undersize fish was not enough for even a modest lunch. "You might as well give it to the cats," Betty suggested. Sandy agreed, though she was doubtful her pampered cats would indulge in anything other than their regular diet of top quality canned food.

"Get in here, guys. I've got a treat for you!" she called. The plump pair of cats stretched themselves awake, ambled into the kitchen, and sniffed the cleaned fish that Sandy had apportioned for each of their dishes. Not a sell. They walked away and looked back as if to say, "Call us if you can come up with anything better."

Sandy's quick mind erupted with a mischievous idea. She reached for the two dishes and placed them out of sight on the counter. She pulled the handle on the can opener and let it run the length of time required to open a can of cat food. She ran it a second time. The cats responded to the familiar rumble of the electric opener and glanced toward the kitchen. Again she placed the two dishes of filleted fish on the cat mat and stepped aside. Both cats hurried to the fresh meal and dug in. Sandy and Betty laughed themselves to tears.

Security is built upon the dependability of order. The sun will rise in the morning. A paycheck will arrive semimonthly. Animals and people are inclined to habits and patterns. But there's a downside to routine. Rigid conditioning stifles flexibility. If we become conditioned to sequences (a can opener must sound before we can eat), we may miss out on something special. Over-conditioning precludes opportunities for new and interesting experiences. Locked in our safe cycles, we may cheat ourselves out of more than a fresh fish lunch.

The Tail End

Break out of your regimen and flex a little!

Service:
Secret to Success

*T*he out-baskets in the offices at city hall in Eagle Point, Oregon, are usually filled with notices, postcards, and memos. At other times, they are occupied by a 12-pound cat. C.C., short for City Cat, is a rotund black and white kitty who pads across the tabletops and patrols the corridors. Like the soccer ball C.C. resembles, he bounces from one desk to another and sometimes naps under the City Council bench. The stray cat made city hall his home about three years ago when he wandered inside and decided to stay. Legal regulations confirmed that no laws forbade the cat's presence. Everyone was glad.

C.C.'s primary service is calming the nerves of workers. The city finance officer describes C.C. as "our stress-reduction specialist." Amidst all the weighty proceedings at city hall, C.C. maintains his unflappable feline cool and shares his composure with harried workers. "If you've had a bad day, you pet the cat," said an employee. C.C. leaps into laps and is seldom refused. The city administrator added, "(C.C.) brings a very soothing factor to the office."

Everyone agrees there is something tranquilizing about the easy manner of this furry fellow.

C.C.'s only misdemeanor occurred the day he posted himself at the computer printer and shredded the outcoming copy. He was scolded and has demonstrated model conduct ever since.

Like other folks, C.C. has his quirks. He drinks from water glasses, never a bowl. Though he enjoys his daytime hours in the prestigious offices, he prefers to spend his nights sleeping outdoors. Police officers oblige C.C. by letting the cat in or out at all hours.

C.C.'s usefulness won him his welcome at city hall. Soon after his arrival he began his ministrations as stress reliever. Service with a smile (or with a meow) is hard to resist even from a stranger. Like City Cat, let's offer ourselves as servants—especially at the place we claim as home. Seeing a need and providing a service will earn you a warm reception anywhere.

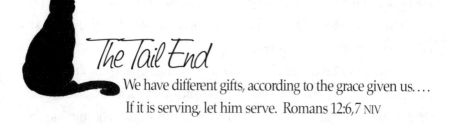

The Tail End

We have different gifts, according to the grace given us....
If it is serving, let him serve. Romans 12:6,7 NIV

Newcomers Welcome

*T*he routine stop at the hardware store was as ho-hum as bathtub caulking and plumbing elbows until Kathy Hamilton and her husband Pat heard the loud meow of a kitten nearby. They selected a few needed items and tried unsuccessfully to ignore the cries. Surely someone in view of the kitten would come to its aid and thus relieve their minds. But the mewing continued and began to cut sharply at their sensitive hearts.

"Jake, you sellin' pets now?" At the check-out stand they overheard a customer inquire of the store owner.

"Nope, but one of my clerks saw a carload of truants dump a box of animals behind the store. I haven't had a chance to check it out. Take a look if you're curious." The owner was too busy to investigate, and the inquirer seemed more anxious to load up his five gallons of house paint than to check on the kitten.

The conversation between Jake and the man was unsettling to the Hamiltons. "I think *we'll* take a look," Pat said as he paid for his purchase. Jake

motioned them to a back door that led into the alley. A rag-tag threesome of Australian mix pups and a forlorn gray kitten hunkered in fright with nowhere to go.

Kathy and Pat wanted to avoid a chase, so Kathy went to the car, grabbed a bag of cold French fries, and enticed each puppy into her husband's quick hands. Even the kitten was hungry enough to devour a slice of salty potato.

The Hamiltons headed back into the store with arms full of fur. Their pass through the aisles attracted many stares from perplexed observers. Jake took one look, figured out what happened, and called out, "I owe you a favor next time you come in, Pat."

Home the whole crew went to join the Hamiltons' five elderly cats. Dog tails wagged happily as Kathy and Pat drove off, but the tiny kitten was scared and starved.

The first job was to wash the entire bevy in flea disinfectant. Shampoo unearthed an all-white kitten who peered at them with one blue eye and one green. Kathy baptized the cat "Rhonda" right there in the soapy waters. Before the evening was over, the Hamiltons, the bathroom tile, the tub and linoleum were completely disinfected as well. The clean team was let loose to run free in the house while Kathy and Pat dried off and began brainstorming about possible homes for the pups. They agreed to keep the kitten.

Their original cadre of five cats chose to remain outdoors, even insisting on meals alfresco until the puppies were gone. The lively dogs spurred Kathy on in her hunt for homes. By the end of the week, one, two, then three homes were located for the pups.

Though Rhonda was being well fed and was visible at times, she had become lost in the background amidst the rambunctious dogs. With the

dogs now gone, Kathy needed to introduce Rhonda to Rose, Scratch, Kitty, Baxter, and Lucy. She feared that her tight-knit family of cats ranging in ages from twelve to sixteen would resent a *mew*-comer. Her observations revealed a satisfying surprise.

The two eldest males experienced a rejuvenation of their nine lives as they supervised, educated, and played with the kitten. Rhonda was the baby, and the mature adults accepted her like an assignment.

For example, one day Kathy saw Scratch leap the fence with a grasshopper kicking between his teeth. Kathy assumed Scratch would tease it on the grass and then snack on the crunchy insect. Instead, he headed straight for Rhonda and dropped it at her feet.

Another incident proving the adult cats' careful vigilance occurred when Rose, the Hamilton's feral feline, delivered an injured mouse to Rhonda, then stayed close by as if to advise Rhonda about the skills of the kill.

Kathy witnessed yet another incident of sibling care. When Rhonda was about a year old, she disappeared for two and a half days. She had never missed a meal since joining the Hamilton family, and was always in the house for the night. Kathy's eldest cat, Kitty, had developed a strong attachment to Rhonda. Though Kitty rarely left the yard, she jumped onto the fence and cried and cried. She leapt down to the front yard and crossed over to the neighbor's lawn, something she had never done before. Kathy was mildly curious, so she followed her. Kitty walked directly to the neighbor's garage door and began rubbing against it. Trapped Rhonda cried her reply. Kathy wrestled the garage door open enough for Rhonda to crawl out. Immediately, "Mama" Kitty took over. She led Rhonda home to a fresh

drink of water and food. Then she groomed her from head to haunch. Soon the two were curled up together asleep in their own back yard.

Kathy was amazed at how her cats received and trained the kitten. No whiskers were bent out of shape when Rhonda joined the group. In fact, things took a better shape for everyone. Rhonda gained a home with five wise mentors, and the aging cats experienced an unexpected revival. No newcomer could have received a kinder reception.

Receiving newcomers will always require give and take—giving of self and kindly accepting the unique attributes that arrive naturally with every person. Our response to new people and things can be joyful or fearful. When we assess the new as an opportunity rather than a threat, there will likely be plenty of pur-r-rks in store.

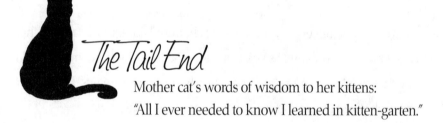

The Tail End

Mother cat's words of wisdom to her kittens:
"All I ever needed to know I learned in kitten-garten."

Someone You'd Yeast Expect

$\mathcal{M}$rs. Cat must have been feeling concern about her physical well-being. The health-conscious Siamese decided to ingest two tablets of brewer's yeast daily. The Schramms, Mrs. Cat's owners, had nothing to do with her decision.

Every night, fifteen-year-old Susan Schramm laid her iron capsule, her thyroid pill, and two brewer's yeast tablets on her bedside table so she would not forget to take them in the flurry of early morning activities. Her doctor had emphasized the importance of an unbroken regimen.

Not long after Susan started this routine, the yeast tablets began to disappear. The first morning she supposed she had accidentally knocked them onto the floor. A search on the rug turned up nothing but an earring. Hurried with collecting her book bag, tennis racket, and poster board project, she gave it little more thought. Grabbing the bottle of yeast, she tipped out two more tablets, swallowed them, and was off to school.

The next morning was a repeat of the previous morning. Susan was both irritated and perplexed. She called to her mom, "I can't believe this! My yeast is gone again!" She and her mother, Kristen, hunted together, this time on hands and knees. Susan's plush carpet was hiding no brewer's yeast. They gave up the search, at least for that morning.

By the third morning, when the yeast was missing again, Kristen had her own theory about the disappearing leaven. "Honey, are you sure you didn't forget to lay them out?" Her mother could think of no other explanation.

"Mom, I know what I do. And this has happened three nights now. There's something going on here. I'm *not* eating them in my sleep."

Off and on for two months the mystery of the vanishing yeast continued. Susan blamed her sister Carol for swiping the tablets, and when she definitively denied it, Susan pointed her finger at little brother Frank. Both were insulted and as curious as she about the strange nightly occurrence.

The following month the yeast disappeared every night. Susan was furious. She certainly did not believe in ghosts. She assumed someone in the family was pulling the annoying prank.

One night Susan awoke at midnight as Mrs. Cat made a silent descent after springing to the foot of Susan's bed. The cat walked straight to the nightstand, selected the yeast with her nose, and chewed up both tablets with zest. Susan threw back the covers, grabbed Mrs. Cat and headed upstairs to her mother's bedroom. "Mom! I caught the robber!" Susan and Kristen both slept better the remainder of the night.

Before school the next day, Frank and Carol learned about the true identity of the yeast thief. They scolded Mrs. Cat for clandestine acts that brought them weeks of undue accusations. Susan apologized for blaming them, and Kristen was relieved that consternation about the yeast would cease to be the breakfast table topic.

For the rest of Mrs. Cat's life (she lived to be twenty!), she dutifully ate two tablets of yeast daily. The yeast helped Susan's complexion and everyone believed it improved the sheen of Mrs. Cat's Seal Point coat.

Swallowing tablets is easier than swallowing a diagnosis of ill health, even for a cat. For this reason, many animal and human treatments include the prescription of natural remedies.

The Schramms were not harsh with Mrs. Cat for confis-cat-ing the yeast. She simply took advantage of what was available—a good lesson for those who live in countries where foods and supplements necessary for good nutrition are in plentiful supply.

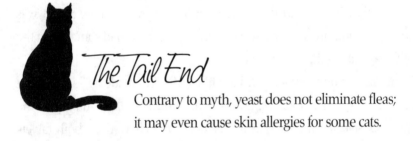

The Tail End

Contrary to myth, yeast does not eliminate fleas; it may even cause skin allergies for some cats.

The Titanic Cat

Some cats choose life on the high seas. Author Mazo de La Roche tells the story of black Cat, born on a coaling ship, who "reigned supreme on the vessel." Indeed, some felines are uncompromisingly sailor cats—some like Jenny.

Jenny's place in seafaring history is even more significant than Mazo's black Cat or even the fictitious pussycat who sailed away in a pea green boat. She will always be remembered as the cat who sailed on the maiden voyage of the *RMS Titanic*.

This feline was no stowaway. Violet Jessop, a *Titanic* stewardess, described Jenny as "part of the crew." Ms. Jessop's memoirs include two paragraphs that tell us all that is recorded about Jenny, the *Titanic* "ship's cat." Much must be left to speculation, but based on known facts about the ship, the voyage, and its passengers, Jenny's own *Titanic* experience was undoubtedly fascinating, remarkable, and tragic.

Jenny was an experienced sailor. Ms. Jessop refers to Jenny's "previous ships," indicating the cat chose sea vessel homes throughout her lifetime.

The steady heaving of the ocean and the swells of storm rocked the cat in her frequent naps across the North Atlantic.

Let us suppose her name, Jenny, was short for Jenni-Fur. Jenny developed a fond attachment to William, a sculleryman (platewasher and kitchen worker). Could it be that Jenny was named after the pregnant wife William left ashore? The large, patient, hard-working scullion, whose eyes did not match and whose good humor was contagious, may have chosen the name in honor of his beloved. Was it William that brought Jenny aboard?

In some way, Jenny managed to obtain passage at the Southampton port and prepared for muster like all crew members that day. Once inside, her sensitive ears heard the toots of six tug boats maneuvering the *Titanic* from her mooring. Jenny then began her search for a "comfortable corner," the words Ms. Jessop used to describe the quarters Jenny selected for herself.

An early discovery Jenny may have made was a dog also sailing on the majestic ship. Did Jenny cringe with disdain each time she caught sight of Henry Sleeper Harper's Pekinese pup strutting the long promenades? She may have thought, "Well! I am owned by a scullion, and I feast on leftovers from hundreds of plates three times a day. What benefits can a passenger's dog boast?"

Actually, Jenny's leftovers would have depended entirely upon William's kitchen assignment. Her menu possibilities were kidney pie and soused herring, entrees served at noon on the day of the launch. Or perhaps William sneaked her the "Sardines à Imperiale" served at dinner that eve.

If Jenny was allowed to roam freely, she may have tiptoed across the rose hue carpets in the first-class reading room and curled in sleep near the

marble fireplace. Cats always find the best places and there were many on the White Star luxuryliner.

Entertainment for Jenny was plentiful. She may have stalked a child's spinning top or enjoyed musical compositions directed by bandmaster, Wallace Hartley.

What conversations did this fated feline overhear? Did she eavesdrop on John Jacob Astor as he discussed the operation of his famed Waldorf-Astoria Hotel? Maybe Jenny's tail brushed the leg of third-class passenger August Sigfrid Carlsson, a twenty-eight-year-old Minnesota-bound Swede, as he spoke of his eagerness to join his brother in the United States.

Jenny may have strolled between the buttoned shoes of the Countess of Rothes. Or listened as Father Thomas Byles recited rosary for those who in the last hour faced the certain doom of the ship.

In truth, we do not know exactly what Jenny saw and did on that ill-fated trip. But Ms. Jessop notes in her account that on one of the four days before the *Titanic's* fatal collision with an iceberg, Jenny gave birth to a litter of kittens in her comfortable corner. Ms. Jessop tells us that Jenny's feline family was situated near William, who gave her a warm devotion. Jenny, unmindful of class divisions, elegant decor, and chef specialties, suckled her young and licked kitten faces whose tightly closed eyes probably never saw the light of life. If indeed Jenny had time to realize the tragedy unfolding on the ship, she must have thought, "If things don't level out, I may need to move my kittens."

During the final moments before *Titanic* was submerged, while the orchestra played "Nearer My God to Thee," like every good mother, Jenny remained with her young.

Jenny was only one of hundreds of mothers aboard, and one of many who lost children or died themselves. While those whose hopes and bodies sank with the lacerated ship, Jenny's devotion was focused upon her kittens. Like the *Titanic*, the glory of man's achievements often sink to the bed of frigid seas, but the glory of motherhood will remain exalted forever.[5,6]

The Tail End

"My mother was the source from which I derived the guiding principles of my life."

John Wesley (Susanna Wesley, mother of John Wesley, had a very large "litter"–sixteen children, ten of whom survived infancy.)

Discovering New Ways

Mom Cat definitely knew better. She had taught her offspring, Bobcat and Tomcat, never to enter a yard with a fenced dog—particularly a big snarling dog. But one morning, Mom Cat mimicked the hypocrite who says, "Do as I say and not as I do." Fangs and feline met in an unfriendly entanglement that left Mom Cat near death. Susan Downes sped her injured and elderly cat to the veterinarian.

"The hind leg is severely damaged, Mrs. Downes; we need to amputate. I know this is an unpleasant option but most cats adjust well with three legs."

Susan struggled to control the trembling in her voice. "That's awful! I can't imagine how she could manage with only three legs. Can't we try something else?"

"The limb will be weak and infection could cause a setback. We can try to save it," said the vet, "but it's not my recommendation." Susan insisted on the less radical treatment. Mom Cat kept her leg. She remained four days at the clinic for medication and supervision and then convalesced at home. The Downes kept

87

her indoors the next few months. Her pleading cries, pawing on the door, and long sessions on the window sill finally convinced Susan to end her isolation.

Mom Cat enjoyed her recovery for only a short time. A few months after her freedom had been restored, a kitten resident in the Downes' home tried to engage her in playful wrestling. Annoyed, Mom Cat jumped from her chair and her unstable leg snapped. Pain provoked a wail of complaint as she limped to a corner. Susan witnessed the incident and knew what lay ahead. The treatment she had dreaded was now inevitable.

Mom Cat sacrificed her entire leg. Susan could hardly believe the vet's prognosis. "You can take her home tomorrow, Mrs. Downes; she'll soon be up and around," he promised. Susan was prepared to bring home a subdued and disgruntled cat. She resisted visions of a pitiful survivor, hobbling, struggling, and enduring the remainder of her few years. But Susan's fears turned out to be unfounded.

The next day she and her husband, John, drove to the clinic to bring Mom Cat home. Susan settled Mom Cat on her lap in the car. No sooner had the engine turned over than the spunky patient scrambled from Susan's grasp, sprung over the front seat, and bounced from one back window to another. "I was aghast! Mom Cat seemed immune to pain, and even more amazing, she was miraculously adaptive. Our pity turned to laughter."

"John, can you believe this?" Susan exclaimed, as Mom Cat grazed John's shoulder and bounded to the front seat. They both marveled at her agility only twenty-four hours after amputation.

Mom Cat returned home with one less leg, but no less dominance among the other cats. As soon as her stitches were removed, she was free to roam again with Bobcat and Tomcat, leading as in the past.

Watching Mom Cat learn new ways to do old tasks was a daily inspiration. Her scratching post had been the gnarled bark of a backyard pine. Sharpening her claws in the traditional way no longer worked. Instead of stretching high with her rear legs lifting her, she learned to sit, and then would dig into the bark as far as her front legs could reach. "She had discovered that claw sheafs loosened just as easily using the new method," said Susan. "Mom Cat was soon routing large dogs out of our yard again. Tomcat and Bobcat would flee at the sight of canine intruders. Not Mom Cat. She remained the protector. My son would shake his head and say, 'That three-legged cat has more pluck than a bulldog.'"

Susan has observed that Mom Cat sometimes returns to her old procedures out of instinct. "When her ear itches, she cocks her head toward the missing leg and pretends to alleviate the tickle. We watch her leg muscles act out the motions that in the past activated her leg to scratch the ear. She never appears frustrated. She completes the futile action, then drops to the floor and rubs her ear against the nearest table leg."

Susan's experience has taught her not to question the recommendations of her vet. But the example of Mom Cat's adaptability has been the most powerful lesson of all. "I think part of the secret to happy adjustment is being content with alternative ways to reach the same ends. I can't help but think of the figurative expression, 'There's more than one way to skin a cat.' As I grow older and lose my ability to accomplish tasks that I've done all my life, I hope I will be as adaptable as Mom Cat. There are a lot of different ways to approach an assignment."

The Tail End

A handicap can be the mother of ingenuity.

The Nurture of Things

*M*issy the cat had no reprieve after weaning her litter of kittens. While she still had milk, she was assigned the care of four needy puppies. Missy nursed the canine litter in loving memory of a dog named Ivy.

The purebred Pomeranian belonging to Jeanette Raulston disappeared two days after giving birth to her puppies. At dawn, Ivy had begged to go out. With whining puppies left in the house, Jeanette expected her back within minutes. One-half hour later Jeanette began looking for Ivy with the help of a flashlight. Jeanette speculated that the circumstances of the dog's disappearance must have been beyond Ivy's control. She would not have abandoned her young.

Jeanette called her daughter and grandchildren who trekked across every foot of their pasture in Medical Lake, Washington, searching for the dog. The only discovery related to Ivy's whereabouts was not a hopeful one. Clues of fur tangled on a rake and surrounded by paw prints suggested a cougar, recently seen by neighbors, may have been involved in Ivy's sudden

disappearance. Jeanette was more inclined to blame the local coyotes who were known for boldly attacking dogs when they were running alongside horseback riders. The plight of the dog with offspring only forty-eight hours old was heartbreaking. "I bawled all morning," said Jeanette.

By eight o'clock that morning, she was faced with the dilemma of feeding the pups. Their hunger directed Jeanette's full attention to finding a nursemaid. The hunt for Ivy would have to continue later. The veterinarian office opened at nine o'clock; Jeanette was waiting in the parking lot before he opened. She hurried back home with eye droppers, miniature bottles, and milk formula. But all the right equipment did not make feeding time a success. Milk spilled onto laps, hands, and puppy chins. Only a small portion reached the growling tummies. Later that day Jeanette discovered that goat's milk went down more easily. Still, the job was unrelenting. The end of one feeding session overlapped into the next. Finding a mother dog became paramount.

After numerous phone calls and inquiries, only one surrogate, of doubtful plausibility, had been suggested. Alicia Wickham was fostering Missy, a Humane Society cat, who had given birth only one month earlier. Alicia was also the owner of Ivy's stud and had been promised the pick of the litter. Jeanette called to tell Alicia, "I'll try to save the pups, but I can't guarantee anything."

Alicia recalled hearing about dogs nursing kittens and cats nursing puppies. She wondered if Missy would cooperate. When she made the decision to offer Missy, her emotions took the lead. "It just makes your heart go out," she said. Alicia noticed Missy had begun to refuse feedings to her kittens. Mother's milk was now a supplement for the kittens; for the puppies it was a dire need. "It wasn't hurting the kittens ... because they were eating cottage cheese already. The puppies needed it more." She telephoned Jeanette to say she was on her way with a lactating cat.

Missy arrived at the Raulston home the evening of that long day. She was resistant and had to be held down for the first feeding. The black and brown Pom puppies, a contrast against Missy's all-white fur, enjoyed forced feedings every ninety minutes until Sunday night. It was then, Missy jumped at will into the blanket-lined box, rolled onto her side, and yielded her teats to the four little whelps. They suckled until they were full. Fulfilling her motherly role, she then licked the puppies clean until they fell asleep.

Jeanette was greatly relieved the puppies were being nourished with mother's milk. "Even though it's from a cat," she said. "I just don't know what I'd do without her." Makayla and Cody, Jeanette's grandchildren, encouraged Missy with affirming strokes and belly rubs.

Three weeks later Missy began the weaning process. When tiny teeth breaking through gums of the growing Pomeranians made nursing uncomfortable, she withdrew. But her lifesaving job was done. Alicia took home her once fostered kitty and formally adopted the heroic cat.

Jeanette decided the location of her home made it too vulnerable for pets. She sold the pups to anxious buyers. As for Missy, her acts were taped on home videos, were featured in the newspaper, and are now recorded in a book.

It was a *happenstance* of nature that Ivy became the unfortunate prey of a wild animal. It was a *happy circumstance* of nature that Missy would nurse a litter of dogs. Though nature is sometimes credited for cruelties, she is also the mother of mercies.[7]

The Tail End

Dear God, I praise You for the countless and touching wonders of nature I behold in the animal kingdom You created. Amen.

One-Time Transient Ascends Throne

*F*riskie bears the first-ever-title of Mr. Catsopolis. The white and black cat was crowned on July 10, 1998. Friskie and his owner, Barb Kietzer of Niles, were awarded a trophy in Cassopolis, Michigan, at the 2,700-acre estate of Ed Lowe, deceased inventor of kitty litter. Other cats received recognition in various divisions while guests sat on hay bales, listened to a lively band, and celebrated with a barbecue.

The day following the cat coronation, a parade honoring Mr. Lowe rolled through downtown streets. Owners of the winning cats rode on the back of a shiny convertible. They held enlarged pictures of Mr. and Ms. Catsopolis who chose to reign in absentia and let their owners share in their glory.

The selection of Mr. and Ms. Catsopolis will likely become an annual event in the small town of 1,822 residents. The town fathers (and mothers) played with the letters in Cassopolis and came up with the kitty rendition, Cats-opolis, an appropriate twist for a town whose patriarch was the first to market absorbent clay to fill kitty litter boxes.

The Cassopolis District Library organized the contest in conjunction with the Ed Lowe festival. Cats were all the hype in Cassopolis, so the library took advantage of the focus. Seventy percent of contest monies were promised to Pets Alive.

The local library published the contest rules. "Entrants must submit an application with a color photo of your cat and a one dollar entry fee. Votes cost ten cents and there is no limit to the number of votes you can cast." Photos were posted on the library bulletin board. Like the forty-eight other contestants who voted for their own cats, Barb admitted she voted for Friskie many times.

The last night of the contest, Barb was disappointed when she received no phone call heralding Friskie's victory. She was sure he had lost—until the next Wednesday morning. "Hello, this is the Cassopolis District Library . . . ," said a cheery voice.

"He won!" Barb shouted before the caller could make her announcement.

"Yes," she said, "but I waited to call until I recounted the votes." Barb ran to find Friskie and told him as well. She was thrilled to learn that the $2,200 collected far surpassed the library's goal.

Friskie, the eight-year-old winner, has one black ear and one pinkish-white ear. Baby pink skin shows underneath his white fur, adding to the frisky guy's rosy image. But life was not always rosy for the feline king.

Having sought warmth and refuge under the hood of a car, the kitten had been taxied from Buchanan to Niles, Michigan, atop the roaring engine. The driver discovered his stowaway and left the cat with the girlfriend he was visiting. It was soon apparent that she was allergic to cat dander, so she gave him to a relative who lived nearby. One night when he was about a year old, he crawled out the window and wandered the neighborhood until Barb, a retired schoolteacher, found him in her back yard.

Friskie was too active for Barb's other two cats, Buster and Sam. Spats were ongoing. A tearful Barb took Friskie to Pets Alive where she has volunteered for ten years. A short time later she adopted old and starving Buddy who had been dumped at the shelter. Buddy was too elderly to care about domination, so he adjusted well to Buster and Sam.

As time passed at the shelter without Friskie's adoption, Barb decided to try him at home once more. Perhaps four cats would be a better blend than three. She was right. The new mix made an amiable quartet.

No worthier person could have been paw-picked as owner of Friskie, the royal cat. Barb's commitment to animals does not stop with her support at Pets Alive. Eight times a year she organizes a bake sale that raises funds for the "no kill" shelter. From September through May she supplements the bake sale proceeds by baking 15 to 20 dozen cookies a week. Every Friday she sells them for a dollar a plate to friends, colleagues, and businesses. Barb was truly delighted when her white and black cat with the raccoon tail was crowned as the first Mr. Catsopolis.

Friskie's lowly beginnings as a vagabond stray did not prevent his later exaltation as the reigning sovereign of Cassopolis. Never doubt the prospects for your future because of a humble past. Every new day offers a fresh opportunity to determine tomorrow's status. If beginnings are modest, they may yet end in coronation. At the same time, fortunate beginnings offer no assurance that life will always be grand unless you continue charting a life course that is worthy of honor.

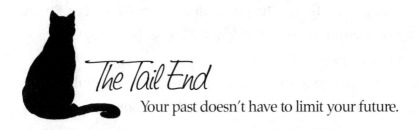

The Tail End

Your past doesn't have to limit your future.

A Leap in the Right Direction

The day of the move from Michigan to Washington was not a cheerful time for Pastor Dave Peterson and his family. The chaos of packing was crisscrossed with painful good-byes and the misery of leaving a house they had loved and lived in for the past seven years.

Transfers from one parish city to another were never easy. This time they were leaving a wonderful community tucked away along the wooded dunes and shoreline of Lake Michigan. Next door neighbors were their children's best friends. Dave had tried to sell the merits of their new home. "Within fifty miles of the city are 75 lakes and several ski resorts." No one was buying it. Grand Haven was home.

The Petersons' two sons and two daughters watched the brawny packers lift, push, heave, and sweat as they loaded possessions into the moving van. Major appliances, sturdy barrels, bed frames and mattresses filled the ample dimensions of the over-sized truck.

Shortly after lunch, the kids noticed their two cats had disappeared. As soon as the movers left, a search began and for the next few hours they looked and called throughout a six-block radius of their house. No cats turned up.

"After the farewell dinner at church, we'll come back and look again," Dave promised. "Yoda and Oreo will probably come back when they see the moving van is gone." He was optimistic.

When they returned from the church that evening, there was still no sign of the cats. Traci sat down on the steps and prayed for help. "Dear God, please say something to us." Immediately, she heard a meow, turned around, and there was Yoda. But no Oreo. The next morning, they exchanged final tearful goodbyes with friends and neighbors, and made one last search for Oreo at the house.

Terri, Dave's wife, had filled a cooler with lunch staples and beverages. The car was loaded with books and travel games, and Dave had highlighted their route on the map. Yoda was boarded among the stuff.

Traci wouldn't get in the car. She sat on the front porch crying while Dave arranged a plan with the neighbors. "Listen honey," Terri explained, "we've got Yoda, and the Suttons have agreed to ship Oreo on the plane as soon as she shows up." It was little comfort but there were no better options. Six people and one cat headed for Washington state.

Oreo's absence compounded the already grievous departure. As if the move was not already difficult enough, a late spring blizzard struck in the middle of their journey. The interstate highway crossing South Dakota closed, stranding them in Sioux Falls for two nights—in sub-zero temperatures. Though they later encountered some beautiful sights, a few

roadside attractions, and new food chains to sample, none of the novelty outweighed nagging concerns about Oreo's welfare. Would she return? Would the Suttons see her if she wandered back? Would she run so far she would get lost? Intermittent crying spells marked the cross-country trip. Even an occasional wail from Yoda indicated he too was anxious about Oreo.

Seven days later they arrived in Washington, stressed and already missing those left behind. They drove to the parsonage soon after the moving van rolled in. The crew then began undoing all of the work from the week before. Out came the prized china cabinet, the aging basement sofa, and stacks of boxes. The exit of beds from the moving van made everyone especially happy. Motel mattresses had not been as heavenly as billboards advertised. The warm feeling of familiarity began to fill the house as belongings were settled into each room.

Yoda was kept in a back room until the last of their goods were unloaded and doors could be closed. Suddenly, the family and movers heard the howling protest of a cat nearby. The cries continued. "It's not Yoda," said Kevin, "he's locked in the bedroom."

As two movers hauled Kevin's box spring into his bedroom, a couple more muffled meows moved along with them. "Sounds to me like that fur ball is in the springs." The burly worker was not fond of cats, and dealing with cat cargo was not routine. He and his partner set down the box springs and hesitated. Then another whine. "Sure enough, that cat's in these springs." A bump underneath the padding hinted at its contents. Huddled in a corner pocket was a cat. Out crawled Oreo!

Squeals of delight welcomed the dehydrated Siamese. Traci was the first to hold her cookie-sweet cat. Oreo had traveled in queen size comfort all the way from Grand Haven, Michigan. Amidst whooping, hollering, and laughter, Oreo was passed from one to another, collecting hugs. They brought her a bowl of water and rummaged through the car for the cat food sack. The reunion was a great beginning to this new chapter in their lives. It seemed to everyone that God was saying, "Welcome home."

At such a happy and grateful moment, Dave could not help but sermonize. "Well, the best way to get where you want to go is to jump on board. Big talk about destinations you hope to reach won't transport you there. The only method for getting where you want to be is to climb aboard the vehicle that will take you. Oreo made a leap in the right direction."

The Tail End

What's the difference between a cat and a comma?
A cat has its claws at the end of its paws and the comma has its pause at the end of its clause.
Source unknown.

Wisdom's Bluff

*T*he name of Cougar totally suited a gutsy little gray tabby owned by a grocer in San Luis Obispo, California. When Vic Deven was a teen, he worked at the grocer's three-man market, stocking shelves and sweeping floors. He soon came to love the owner's furry associate. The store sat three car widths from the highway at the edge of town. The open-front building displayed seasonal fruits and vegetables to entice passersby. One summer day Vic stood at the entrance and witnessed an incident he will always remember.

Cougar sat underneath the fruit stands. From that vantage point she enjoyed a view of the highway, north and south, and was shielded from footsteps of shoppers. There the rising sun warmed her bones and glorified the sheen of her silver stripes.

Mid-morning that day, six boys around seven years old approached the store. Before the era of supermarkets and television, children enjoyed a common delight on summer weekends. With a few precious pennies, they

headed for the nearest grocer to buy candy. Playing follow-the-leader, a spectacled boy led the youngsters in a single file march. In prancing step behind the last follower was a panting collie, also relishing the game. The procession reached the entrance and the boys entered. But the dog spied Cougar and broke forth in a vicious vocal oration. The owner heard the ruckus and sent Vic to investigate. "Why don't you see what all that fuss is about?"

Vic walked only as far as the top step, where he had a panoramic view of the confrontation. By now, the noisy collie was face-to-face with Cougar. Unlike most cats in a similar predicament, Cougar never flinched. Her ears were upright, her back was not arched, and she looked at the dog with utter contempt. Even when the emboldened collie moved his long nose only inches from Cougar's eyes, the cat did not budge.

Adding to the dog's perplexity, Cougar then turned her head as far to the left as possible, and casually surveyed the road. "Yip, bark, bark! Woof!" The dog kept up his clamor. Then Cougar looked to her right, to observe the view at her opposite side, while ignoring the dog's hot breath and cool insults. Vic noticed only one hint of Cougar's discomfort. The tip of her tail flitted in a subtle expression of irritation. And so, each animal persisted in a stance—the dog acting ferocious, the cat acting bored.

Cougar's nonchalant disinterest must have baffled the collie. If dogs could talk, he might have said, "Something's just not coming together here!"

Though Vic watched, ready to intervene, Cougar needed no assistance. The duped dog was bluffed. In comic brisk backsteps, the collie moved 20 feet toward the highway pavement, though never diminishing his vocal performance nor turning his eyes from Cougar. He then paused, but continued his canine cantata while Cougar continued her left and right gazes.

With fists clutching hard candies, stick candy, and taffy, the youthful patrons ran out of the store and called to the dog. "C'mon Sandy!" The collie fell in line once again, still barking and occasionally glancing back in wonder at his unruffled quarry.

When the episode ended and the dog's voice was finally muffled from the roar of a passing car, Cougar looked at Vic as if to say, "It takes all kinds!"

Who knows what would have befallen Cougar had she fought or tried to flee when the intimidations began? Instead, she held her position, concealed her fear, and wisely bluffed herself through a potentially hazardous confrontation. Sometimes a false display of fearlessness will nurture *true* confidence. It is a technique of courage, not of deception. It worked for Cougar. It may work for you.

The Tail End

Cat protocol allows for snubbing.

Double Dozen Rescue

"R.N. Rescues and Treats 24 Survivors," is a headline one might expect to read about a registered nurse with a big heart. But the true story behind nurse Georgia Konstantakos's heroic effort is about the salvage and treatment of twenty-four feral cats.

When Georgia learned about a part-time supervisor position at Mirada Hills Convalescent Home in Whittier, California, the medical-surgical nurse decided to reduce her hours and accept the job. Her employment turned out to be a double calling—a ministration to recovering patients, and the rescue of wild cats who resided near the facility.

Soon after beginning her new job, Georgia learned about the cats. One group claimed the territory around the main building and lived on provisions offered by the elderly Dutch cook. Another group roamed the area surrounding the laundry building.

Georgia was astounded by the large number of wild cats and kittens. The kitchen staff called some by name. These were stick-to-the-description

style monikers: Blackie, B & W (Black and White), Tiger, Stripes—nothing distinguished, like Henry or Alexa. They were homeless beggars, grateful for the generic brand cat food that filled their dishes daily.

When Georgia broached her idea about capturing the cats, the staff encouraged her. But she suspected she would need help.

She called a good friend who was a volunteer at a pet rescue organization. "Sharon, you won't believe what's going on at the place where I'm working!" Georgia explained the situation and the two friends decided they would attempt to trap the cats, have them spayed, and tame them for adoption—not an easy undertaking.

On Georgia's days off, she and Sharon took lawn chairs, potato chips, sodas, and humane traps to the convalescent home and sat quietly from 11:00 p.m. until 2:00 a.m. listening for the snap of a trap signaling the capture of a cat. During the next three months, a few critters other than cats investigated the tuna and chicken bait. One early morning, Georgia and Sharon discovered their quarry was an opossum. "Sharon and I are terrified of 'possums. Once I was bitten by one. They have fifty-two teeth, you know!" she added. "We tilted the cage this way and that, to release the 'possum without becoming victims of an attack. That particular morning we did a lot of squealing!" she said.

One by one, and sometimes two by two, the wild felines were caught and taken to the vet. After the doctor was apprised of the operation and had handled six or seven of the barely manageable cats, he began reacting with a tinge of reluctance when Georgia arrived with newly filled carriers. "Not another wild one, Georgia!" In truth, he supported the endeavor and the spay campaign which Georgia financed entirely from her own pocket.

Though twenty-four cats were initially collected, among them were two pregnant queens whose offspring added to the total. Georgia's house had designated rooms for wild and semi-tame cats. Once home, the savage cats were kept in one of two places. Most of them were restricted to the back bedroom for as long as three months before Georgia transferred them to the "Cat Room." They jumped up the walls and balanced themselves on top of picture frames. "Friends didn't believe me until they saw it for themselves. All the ribbons won by my show cat were torn from the walls and I had to remove all my Garfield collector plates so they didn't get broken." It took eight to ten months to tame them. Through a pet rescue group called "Love-A-Pet," most of the cats were adopted.

The only physical effects Georgia suffered during the rescue operation was a case of mange, a disease which is characterized by skin lesions, itching, and loss of hair. She contracted the parasites from Scruffy, a cat who nearly died from the disease.

The rescue effort is now complete. Georgia ended up keeping only six of the twenty-four cats from the convalescent home. Her back yard is enclosed with netting to contain her current aggregate of twenty-two cats. Though domesticated, none of Georgia's lair are lap cats. Someone once asked her if it was disappointing to invest so much time and love in animals who reciprocate so little. "I love them regardless," she said. "Every day I do a head count, which says something about my affection for them. And I think they care for me. Each one responds to its name."

However, Georgia says she has drawn the line. "Twenty-two is a good number. I think I'll stop here." Though her cats still get more sleep than she,

Georgia is no longer living on the wild side. She has returned to full-time nursing and continues caregiving to her live-in mother.

Georgia proudly reports that the few remaining "wild ones" at the convalescent home are spayed, and no kittens have been born for many months. "I think the community is under control," she said. "That was our goal." Periodically, she delivers a barrel mix of coupon-special cat food to the cook who still feeds the remaining cats. Though Georgia is no longer a nurse supervisor, she will always be supervisor-at-large to a small society of cats in Whittier.

There are many sad and desperate conditions worldwide. Few of us have resources or adequate time to halt every activity that is out of control. But like Georgia, we can select a representative problem, commit ourselves for a season, and eliminate the progression of unrestrained evil in some small place.

The Tail End

Begin helping the world by first helping your neighborhood.

Thera-Pet

*R*ebecca Causey established an attitude of professionalism in her approach to setting up her home business. In the beginning, she denied her cat, Sunny Delight, access to her office. The massage therapist, who lives in Greensboro, North Carolina, felt that a lounging cat in the patient cubicles did not fit her concept of professionalism. But she soon learned that her two-year-old butterscotch tabby also had his own career in mind.

Sunny Delight has massage expertise of his own. With permission, he leaps onto backs, treads across shoulders and sometimes offers a feline knead of the gluteals and hamstrings. One client told Rebecca she should charge extra for cat therapy. Nearly everyone regards Sunny Delight as a qualified member of the business.

Every day begins before business hours with the same client, Sunny Delight himself. The eleven-pound feline is a believer in the therapeutic value of massage. After Sunny's breakfast, Rebecca massages his body this way and that, indulging her pet. "Unlike some of my clients whose muscles

are resistant to massage techniques, Sunny Delight yields to my methods and thus gets the full benefit of my skills. He's as moldable as a bag of rice."

The cat's inclination to massage people is not unusual to his species. When kittens nurse, they press on the teats of the dam to stimulate milk flow. As they suckle, their tiny paws maintain a piston-like rhythm. Even bottle-fed kittens knead, pressing on human hands that hold the bottle and on surrogate parents who care for them. Adult cats knead both their owners and inanimate objects like blankets or bed pillows.

Most people acquainted with cats view this peculiar action as affectionate and welcome, although it may feel prickly when claws are untrimmed. Kittens who are separated too soon from their mothers, grow up to be "adult kneaders," like Sunny Delight, more commonly than kittens who enjoyed normal weaning periods. Sunny Delight, now an adult, works out his "too early weaning" frustrations on Rebecca's willing clientele. Pink pads knead tense muscles and aching joints.

Though a cat lover, Rebecca first began her practice without cats. One of her clients asked her to take an elderly stray who showed up at her home. Rebecca reluctantly accepted Miss Piggy. Sixteen months later, Shadow Box, another stray, arrived in Rebecca's wood pile. Now she had two cats. Though the two cats sometimes went into her offices, they were unobtrusive in their demeanor and hardly noticed by clients. Sometime later the aging Miss Piggy passed away. A client arrived one day and began pressing her to take one of the three kittens from a deserted litter she had rescued and bottle-fed. "Shadow needs a companion," her client reasoned.

Rebecca declined but promised to go see the kitten after she returned from her vacation. After one look at the undersized eight-week-old kitten, she fell in love. It soon became plain that Sunny Delight would not be a demure and inconspicuous cat like his predecessors. He quickly became a participant in the business.

Only a few times have potential clients declined the practitioner's services because of the cat. One lady was allergic to cats and appreciated Rebecca informing her of Sunny Delight's assistantship.

Another time, Rebecca was concerned about the reaction of an immaculately groomed client who came weekly. How would the businesswoman react if Sunny left cat hair on her costly attire? Sunny Delight always ran to her the moment he heard her footsteps. Rebecca tried to catch him before he rubbed against her silky hosiery but seldom succeeded. But Rebecca's concerns were needless. The elegantly appareled woman would sweet-talk him as soon as he appeared. She always enjoyed his obvious attraction to her. They became great friends.

The intrusion of her cat among her clients was the very thing Rebecca had tried to avoid. Contrary to her fears, the massaging kitty has become her sidekick, greeter, comforter, and mood lifter. If he is gone, clients often inquire, "Where's Sunny Delight, today?"

Rebecca did discover one liability with having a cat associate. She must endure Sunny Delight's attitude about business hours. Some days he does not show up at all. His leaves of absence are particularly noticeable in the summertime. He naps on his cat furniture, suns himself outdoors, studies the tropical fish tank, or plays with his toys. If Sunny Delight could talk, he would probably defend himself with the suggestion that his time off is part of the healthy lifestyle he emulates for clients. After all, one must balance work life with exercise, entertainment, and rest.

The Tail End

Why is it that a fickle person is judged undependable and loses respect while the always fickle cat is judged as merely unpredictable and retains his dignity?

Whitey Proves His Worth

$\mathcal{L}$iving through the Great Depression of the 1930's left an indelible mark on Charlotte Huskey. Her family, like hundreds of others in Oklahoma City, was left without resources or steady employment.

"Able-bodied men were expected to do any kind of work to support their families. Proprietors kept records of debts, and in some cities, amounts charged against a person were posted in the town's annual report," Charlotte explained. With no job and little hope of finding one, few people wanted to incur debt and have their debts publicized for neighbors to read. For that reason, most folks preferred to starve or survive on little rather than ask help from the welfare system.

"Dad shoveled snow, split wood, washed windows, and worked on roads for a dollar a day. Often he accepted food in return for day-long jobs. He searched for work until his feet were blistered. Our family's main diet was bean or pea soup with biscuits and water gravy, a bland sauce made without meat broth or milk." Consequently, the idea of an extra animal to feed on the farm was out of the question.

When Charlotte's brother, Jimmy, brought home Whitey, a short-haired kitten, their father immediately objected. "Son, we can't have a cat. I can't fill all our mouths now, and we don't need a cat reproducing herself around here."

Jimmy was crushed. Like many ten-year-old boys, he longed to keep the fluffy white kitten. As if it was a very sensitive matter, little Charlotte, then five, and Jimmy toted the kitten out of sight and lifted his tail for a confirmation exam, then sighed with relief when his gender proved to be male. They ran back to their father to plead again. "It's a boy, Dad. Don't have to worry about more kittens. And if we don't feed him he'll know he has to mouse. Pleas-s-s-e, can we keep him?"

The tenderhearted father hated to deprive his children of a pet when they were already having to do without so many other things. "Okay, but I better not catch you feedin' that cat; he'll do fine on his own." Charlotte and Jimmy promised, but more than once they slipped a snitch of bread or a saucer of milk to the hungry cat.

"We looked upon most of our animals as pets," remembered Charlotte, "but they also became food sources. Our female calves and goats provided milk, and a few males were butchered for meat. Even our horses served us through labor, but we never regarded the dogs or our past cats as more than companions. That is, until Whitey."

One winter morning, Charlotte's mother, Mabel, awoke early as Whitey scratched at the door. In dread of the morning hours when the house was icy cold, she was reluctant to climb from the bed. She supposed the strong Oklahoma winds were rattling the door. But the noise persisted until she

realized it was Whitey. By then, he was alternating his scratching with loud meowing. Mabel dreaded tripping through the frigid house, and she knew she would face a snowdrift when she went to let in Whitey. She turned over and covered her ears.

Whitey continued. Mabel finally gave in, wrapped herself in a robe and marched to the door while mumbling, "That cat! What an hour to be demanding!"

She opened the door just a crack, and there on the snow-covered porch lay a large cottontail rabbit. Whitey was standing guard to keep the neighbor's dog from stealing it.

Mabel snatched up the rabbit in one arm and Whitey in the other. Whitey had dined on the head, but a plump body remained. She laid the still warm rabbit on the table, hugged Whitey and stroked his back as she laughed and then cried. Weeks had passed since there had been meat on the table.

Mabel skinned and prepared the rabbit for breakfast. "What a surprise to awake that morning to the aroma of cooking meat," said Charlotte. "Of course, Jimmy was never more proud of his cat."

"What I remember most was Dad's reaction. He dressed, gathered our family together, and asked us to bow on our knees for grace. 'Thank You, God, for supplying food for my family,' he managed to pray until his voice broke. My father, always a faithful Christian, that morning was a very grateful Christian."

The rest of the winter, Whitey regularly brought home rabbits. A few times he delivered rats, for which Mabel praised him, but it was the rabbits that were eaten. As a result of Whitey's provisions, the family developed a life-long love for rabbit meat.

"Dad seldom paid attention to Whitey until he began supplying rabbits. After Whitey proved his worth, Dad treated him with respect and kindness. Maybe Whitey realized Dad had made a concession in offering him shelter," Charlotte surmised. "Whitey demonstrated his appreciation by giving back and, in so doing, demonstrated God's care for our family. Whitey's service and the rabbits' sacrifice met our needs that hard and lean winter of 1939."

"The next spring Dad share-cropped near Del City. Years later he bought a farm in the fertile Williamette Valley of Oregon. There we had lots of animals and once again, we made pets of most of them. Dad lived on the farm until he was too old to work. He used to say, 'I need to be where I can grow crops and raise stock in case another depression hits. I may never have another cat like Whitey.'"

The Tail End

I know what it is to be in need, and I know what it is to have plenty. I have learned the secret of being content in any and every situation, whether well fed or hungry, whether living in plenty or in want. Philippians 4:12 NIV

He Knew All Along

*C*rystal named her kitten after precisely what she looked like—Cinders. Her black and gray coat was thick and long. "When you reached for Cinders you felt like you needed first to brush ash dust from her tiny body," Crystal remembered. "I called her Cindy for short."

When Crystal studied, Cindy would begin in Crystal's lap, but usually ended up sprawled over books, binders, and notes, not subtle in her bid for attention. Crystal dressed Cindy in doll clothes and pushed her along in a buggy. Though the kitten was not technically allowed in the house, Crystal's eleven-year-old imagination contrived incontestable reasons to bring her indoors. Cindy and Crystal were inseparable. Sometimes her mother referred to the two as "the girls."

Soon Cindy was old enough to be fixed. Crystal was perplexed by the term "fixed." In her judgment, Cindy was perfect—nothing about her needed improvement, much less repair. Crystal's mother explained that

Cindy would undergo a procedure called spaying to prevent her from conceiving kittens.

Mel Oliver, Crystal's army sergeant father, took Cindy to the free military veterinary clinic. After completing required forms that recorded the animal's name, sex, and other pertinent information, Mel waited until the operation was completed.

Eventually, the doctor poked his head around a corner and told Mel, "I'd like to talk with you privately before sending Cindy home, Sergeant Oliver."

"Is the cat all right?" Mel suspected something had gone awry.

"Yes, but I need to have a brief discussion with you," he explained.

A few minutes later, the tall doctor stepped out smiling and announced that Cindy would fully recover, but said her surgery had turned out to be more extensive than routine spaying.

"You see, Sergeant, Cindy has an extra incision. We operated on your cat understanding he was a female. But Cindy is a male. We closed up the extra incision when no female organs were present. This happens seldom more than once in the lifetime practice of veterinarians. It's my first and I hope my last mistake of this kind. It shouldn't have happened and we apologize for putting Cindy through the unnecessary trauma."

Everyone was chagrined—the veterinarian, his staff, and Mel. On the drive home, Mel pondered the regrettable and embarrassing but humorous outcome. Neither he nor Crystal's mom had thought to confirm the cat's sex, and Crystal had never checked to determine if her beloved Cinders was a boy or a girl! Of course, *he* knew all along.

"The joke was on us but the situation was no joking matter for the stitched up kitten," said Crystal. "In fact, we immediately changed his name to

Joker. At first it was hard remembering to call Cinders 'him and he,' but both we and the cat got used to the change. The clinic had no boarding facilities, so Dad had to bring Joker home while he was partly under the anesthesia. We agonized as we watched Joker's first unsteady steps and his struggling effort to reach the door. Over the next few days, we cared for him in earnest, and like the veterinarian promised, he soon recovered."

In the years that followed Joker's surgery, he often acted like the tough guy he really was. In an incident Crystal's mom will always remember, a little bulldog entered the yard and suddenly began to yelp, "Ki-yi, ki-yi-yi!" She looked, and there was Joker, riding the back of the dog, in cow-BOY style, as the dog tried to flee. Joker was not easily daunted and he had scars to prove it!

In the same way that Joker suffered the consequences of a medical mistake, innocent people become victims of the mistakes of others. Joker's veterinarian was an experienced professional, but he was human. Blunders and foul-ups happen even when precautions are established to prevent them. Being human means living in a world where we are vulnerable. If we are as resilient as Joker, we will heal. When we suffer damage from someone else's folly, our best response is to realize that we too are error-prone.

The Tail End

Seventy thousand dogs and cats are born every day because of uncontrolled breeding. Seventy-five percent of cats entering shelters are euthanized. Control the cat population by spaying your pets and encourage your friends and neighbors to do the same.[8]

Forbear the Feeble

When J. Dave Siddon, founder and director of an animal rehabilitation center, watched a grizzly bear meet a 10-ounce kitten, there was no doubt in his mind what the outcome would be. The kitten was the last among a litter of four who were deserted that summer at Wildlife Images Rehabilitation and Education Center, in Grants Pass, Oregon. Volunteers succeeded in trapping the other three kittens and found homes for them. But this kitten wandered into the pen only to jeopardize its life in the enclosure of a 650-pound bear.

The brown bear, named Griz, had lived at the rehabilitation center from the time he was an eight-month-old cub. While foraging on railroad tracks in Montana, Griz, his mother, and his sister were hit by a train. Both mother and sister were killed in the collision. Griz sustained major head and shoulder injuries that eventually healed, but he could never be returned to the wild. Two months in intensive care left him comfortable with humans and

therefore unsafe in the wild. Siddon described Griz as the "gentlest, sweetest thing you ever saw. He's sort of the Forrest Gump of bears."

However, even gentle and sweet beasts can be testy at mealtime. When Dave spotted the kitten in the bear's pen, Griz was lunching from his five-gallon bucket of kibble, meat, fruit, vegetables, and road-kill venison. Dave almost panicked. "I thought the bear would swat him and kill him. Grizzlies are omnivorous, you know. They'll eat baby fawns, baby moose, baby elk, baby beaver." Dave remained quiet and simply watched, not wanting to excite the bear. He dreaded the worst for the six-week-old orange kitten.

To his complete amazement, the most remarkable thing happened. The immense bear pulled a chicken wing from his food bucket and dropped it by his forepaw for his small visitor. The kitten, too hungry to hesitate, snatched it and ran into the blackberry thickets to eat the share offered by the great and gracious host.

Griz's hospitality was interpreted by Cat, (so named by the center's employees) as an invitation to visit again in Griz's half-acre wooded home. Thus began their unnatural affiliation.

Their relationship became obviously amicable, even affectionate. The cat slept curled up under the chin of the bear. Griz often picked up the cat by the nape of his neck and carried him around. Dave said, "Cat would lie in ambush, then leap out and swat Griz on his nose. Sometimes Griz licked Cat." Though Cat came and went as he pleased, as he grew older, he spent more of his time with the bear. Dave admired the pair's extraordinary friendship. "It's an example of Mother Nature at her best."

As Griz resisted his instinct to dominate his food supply and doffed his natural inclination to protect his territory, he gained a friend in an otherwise

lonely environment. Only when we exercise gentleness toward the impoverished and offer assistance to the weak, will we discover the compensations that await us as benefactors. Griz knows.

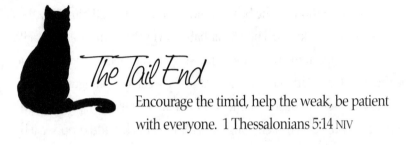

The Tail End

Encourage the timid, help the weak, be patient with everyone. 1 Thessalonians 5:14 NIV

The loving friendship between Cat and Griz was second only to the bond Griz shared with Dave Siddon himself. In October 1996, Mr. Siddon, who played with Griz almost every day, died of cancer. Griz's emotional trauma from the loss of his owner was immediately obvious to workers at the center. But medical tests revealed nothing physically wrong with the bear, other than his recurring arthritis. A little over one year after Mr. Siddon's death, Cat also disappeared. Now the two most significant companions in Griz's life were absent forever. In late August 1998, several months after Cat's disappearance, the nearly nine-year-old bear was discovered dead in his pen. Workers are convinced he died of a broken heart.

Between the Covers

"Never judge a book by its cover," echoes the old adage. Employees at the used bookstore, Twice Sold Tales, apply the saying to their business in Seattle, Washington. "Don't presume you know what's between our walls until you visit," says Jamie Lutton, owner-manager of the downtown establishment.

As surprising as the contents of some books, is the discovery of six feline residents inside the store. Lisa Maslowe, store employee and self-declared spokesperson for the cats, says, "The cats have as varied personalities as the characters in our novels." Even if buyers occasionally purchase a dull book, they find nothing dull about the company of cats who enjoy the shelter and love at the bookstore.

The stories the cats enact are filled with elements that make suspenseful reading. Intrigue, rivalry, rejection, jealousy, and deception create scenes that *usually* conclude in satisfying resolutions.

Sissy, a black and orange tortoiseshell, prefers to play the antagonist in the feline dramas. She loves to be spanked at the base of her spine, but loathes to

be petted and is violent with anyone who offers a kindly-intentioned stroke. She enjoys sitting beside the cash register where patrons must be warned, "Don't pet the cat!" Few heed Lisa's caveat, until a hand is torn by six sharp claws. This kitty boasts six toes on each of her four large feet.

Nesbit, a six-year-old red tabby, has lived at the store the longest but his origin is unknown. Plainly the dominant cat, he often asserts himself in testy style. He held strong dislike for Sissy's mother who was finally removed from the store due to Nesbit's animosity. Though the leader, Nesbit's melancholy temperament became noticeable when his status was threatened by another male feline added to the company. He withdrew under a stairway and moped for a month. But what is a good story without a character who displays a bit of psychosis?

Nevada, a tortoiseshell Manx with lime green eyes, is regarded as the smartest of the cats. She usually keeps to herself unless she is soliciting a chase through the store aisles, her favorite game.

Mama Cat brings deception to the feline troupe. She arrived conveying the impression that her swollen tummy was cradling kittens. She was assigned a quiet back room with a box for nesting. Mama Cat ate, and ate, and ate, but never gave birth. They took her to the vet who informed them she had long ago been spayed, and could more appropriately be renamed Fat Cat. Strangely, this cat with the bulging belly exercises more than any of the others.

Marmite is a handsome lady's man who adds a touch of romance to the storyline. The black short-haired Burmese is sleek and panther-like. His pulchritude instantly attracted Pandora, a visiting female who had been deserted at the store one day. Pandora was at first unapproachable and frightened by her new surroundings. She hid under the front counter for two

days. Then she emerged, suddenly amorous! She rolled on her back and enticed Marmite under the counter. Pandora was in heat! Employees partly dismantled the counter and poked the love-struck pair with a broom until they were extri-cat-ed, then swiftly escorted them to a spay-neuter clinic!

Buster, a Siamese-mix, was a two-week-old kitten when Jamie took the wee orphan. Someone rescued him from the middle of the street after being alerted by a barking terrier who stood close by. Jamie bottle-fed him and nursed him through a serious illness. "I have no children," she said, "and this kitty was my baby. I fed him every three hours around the clock the first few weeks."

Friendly Buster loves children and likes to nurture the litters of kittens brought to the store. Reputed for its "placement service," the store has located carefully screened homes for ninety kittens. Though well-adjusted, Buster seems to be the least intelligent of the cats. "We call him the 'The Wonder Cat,'" said Lisa, "because as a previous employee used to say, 'we wonder about him!'"

The blackest moment in this tale of six cats was the day Buster was cat-napped. Jamie posted a reward for one hundred dollars and grieved through a week long wait. At last, Buster was returned, though clueless as ever.

Protagonists and antagonists alike advance the story at Twice Sold Tales, but there are no minor characters. Each of the cats is important in the bookstore saga. Jamie and the employees value the cats enough to provide some fancy commodities for them.

For example, a two-foot by three-foot hammock drapes between bookshelves for the comfort of the frequent cat nappers. Spiral ladders lead to ramps that run along the tops of the bookshelves, providing a cat's eye view of the mercantile twenty-four hours a day. Portholes between rooms are cut above the ramps, allowing the cats to move from room to room without getting under foot of shoppers. Another of the bookstore features that cats (and clientele) enjoy are the night sales. Once a week from midnight until eight o'clock in the morning, book prices are reduced 25 percent. Nocturnal by nature, the cats enjoy the all-night traffic of shoppers.

Twice Sold Tales and six bold tails relate endless stories at the busy secondhand bookstore. Typical of life, the cats symbolize authentic relationships, tragedies, and victories that summarize real life for cats and humankind alike. Indeed, life is stranger than fiction. Lisa says the cats are now living happily together. Like all good story finales, she hopes it will be "forever after."

The Tail End

Lord of my heart, help me remember through the dismal scenes of my life, that "happily ever after" awaits me in the final chapter. Amen.

Part of the Design

$\mathcal{I}$n 1961, on a farm in Perthshire, Scotland, a shorthaired cat with folded ears, named Susie, gave birth to a litter of kittens. Two in the litter had forward folding ears, giving the appearance of a close fitting cap. The pair became the foundation stock for the Scottish fold breed.

Carolleone Eres, Scottish fold breeder said, "I'm in fashionable company. Even Calvin Klein owned a fold." Carolleone is plainly partial to the breed. Her favorite fold was her own Sandy McTavish.

"Sandy was a beautiful specimen of the earliest folds," said Carolleone. Classic to the breed, Sandy's velvet coat was so thick it did not part when blown upon. His sturdy body was marked by a red saddle and white face on the typical melon-shaped head with large round eyes that were wide-set. He waved a short tail, walked on huge feet, and wore the distinct folded ears. With characteristic short legs, "he looked like he was cut off at the knees," Carolleone remarked. "When you reached for Sandy, you'd wonder

where to grab him. The folds have thick necks; they're as hard to grasp as a plump little pig."

Folds are friendly, playful, and mild-tempered. As kittens, these cats are superb with children but they quickly turn into bean bags as adults; they are just not as interactive or demanding as other breeds like the Siamese. Their other unique habit is head butting. Unlike other cats that rub with their head or cheek, folds butt like a goat.

No picture of a fold would be complete without a description of a peculiar sitting position they often assume. With their upper spine propped against furniture or a wall, they rest the lower part of their body on their haunches with legs stretched forward. The focal point of the pose is their tummy. The posture is similar to that of a full-bellied Buddha.

Another unusual trait of folds caused the breeder and her fold buyers a scotch of consternation and unnecessary expense. X-rays of the Scottish folds reveal their palate is more akin to a canine's mouth than a feline's. The design of the nasal passages causes the cats sporadically to exhale a mucous discharge, alarming owners with the suspicion that the cat may be ill. Thus, Carolleone advised all her buyers to take their cats to a veterinarian she recommended who was well informed about the breed.

Nonetheless, a few customers called her in distress, sure their cats were suffering from rhinotracheitis, a contagious viral infection, or some other malady. "My fold is sick. Did you know the cat was ill when you sold her to me?" Buyers asked pointed questions. Though Carolleone had explained the fold tendency at the time of purchase, they had forgotten and were ready to rush their cats to the vet.

"Did you take your fold to Dr. Watkins?" Carolleone would always ask.

"No, I have a vet I trust." They were sure their family vet was fully apprised of breed anomalies. But the puffing Scots were being escorted to veterinarians who were not educated about the strange symptom.

Later visits to Dr. Watkins by worried owners confirmed their cats were healthy. The fold specialist echoed Carolleone's explanation. She said no buyers returned their lad or lassie folds because of the nasal feature—they grew to accept the anomaly as part of the fold design.

Even beyond the animal world, deviations from the norm can be viewed in two ways—as inherent to the design or as defects. Even clothing is sometimes accompanied by a tag noting that the slubs (irregular bumps) in the thread or yarn are not flaws, but rather are typical of the fabric. If we can love cats that blow and dogs that drool, why do we have such a hard time loving people with eccentricities? A gracious way to overlook harmless personality quirks is to regard them as slubs—not as defects that are cause for rejection, but as traits that endear us to a person.

The Tail End

I praise you because I am fearfully and wonderfully made; your works are wonderful, I know that full well.
Psalm 139:14 NIV

Frequent Flyer

A flying feline missed only one flight during his more than 90,000 miles of travel during the Pacific Campaign in World War II. He confused the sound of the engines on an Army Air Corps plane with those of the aircraft he co-piloted with Captain Ed Stelzig of the 5th Squadron, Second Combat Cargo Group. The cat hopped aboard the wrong plane and ended up 500 miles from his owner-pilot's destination.

In 1945, cat and Captain had met at an unlikely venue. Stelzig was commissioned to Darwin, Australia, to transport a group of officers on leave. While the pilot was resting on the tarmac in the shadows of the wings, the black and white stray jumped into his lap. The affectionate kitten purred himself into the heart of the war-weary soldier. Stelzig decided to keep the kitten. Later, he put food and a litter box at the rear of the plane, and from that day on, the conscripted cat accompanied the pilot on all his missions but one.

The cat's unusual markings and the country's archenemy influenced the choice of a name for the kitten. His head was mostly white except for

a small black patch beneath his nose shaped like the moustache of the German dictator, Adolf Hitler. Everyone who saw the tiny feline agreed that a fitting name would be Adolf.

Adolf became Stelzig's honorary co-pilot. He suffered no ill effects from altitudes, and loved to sleep on the warm radio equipment. At the end of each assignment, the cat would leap from the plane, explore the airstrip and not return until he heard the familiar whine of the engines revving up on Stelzig's plane.

One day Adolf heard the roaring engines of another plane, and sprang aboard, unnoticed. What a surprise to the crew when they discovered their pussycat passenger. It must have been an equal surprise for Adolf when he realized he was separated from Stelzig. Eventually, the cat and captain were reunited. Adolf never made that mistake again.

When the war the over, Stelzig received his orders to return home. He presented Adolf to the children of a retired colonel. They adored the flying feline—a veteran of war who logged 92,142 airborne miles.

Even with a cat's keen sense of hearing, it can still make mistakes like Adolf when he mistook the engines of another plane for Stelzig's. Though cats begin to lose their auditory abilities around the age of five, they hear many times better than humans. Cats have forty thousand fibers in their aural nerve while humans have thirty thousand. In spite of natural endowments, cats and humans are liable to err.

Mistakes sometimes divert our intended direction. Some are even irreversible. But most mistakes can be instruments of education and teach us cautionary principles for the future. Adolf failed to discern the correct engines and was flown yonder through skies 500 miles from his owner. But with the help of others, he managed to rechart a flight back to Stelzig.

An occasional mistake in judgment need not keep us off course forever. A far worse mistake is in refusing to correct it.[9]

The Tail End

Abraham Lincoln rescued three young cats that he found half-frozen in General Grant's camp during the Civil War.

Dumpster Deliverance

$\mathcal{A}$leece and her sister, Nelle, have never considered themselves heroines. But in the green, blue, and amber eyes of a dozen or so cats, they match the definition. A rescue operation they initiated with the Okefenokee Humane Society in Dixie Union, Georgia, places them in the cat-egory of heroines, particularly in the eyes of cat lovers.

The sisters have tender hearts for "throw-aways," as they call them. Whenever they find a deserted feline, they have it neutered or spayed, vaccinated, and then they find a home in need of a perfect pet. That's how they ended up with twelve cats, only one of which they purchased. This bargain cat was bought for a few dollars from the owner who threatened to "get rid of her." Aleece and Nelle offered the woman a five dollar bill, and left with a gem of a kitten they named Ruby.

Their most recent adoptee was discovered at a nearby creek and is enjoying playing kitten to Pierre, also a newcomer. There's Harley, and Scotland, a cat from the woods who is a splendid Maine Coon look-alike.

Keatsie is a grey and white Manx, and there is Golden who brought her two offspring, Atilla the Hun and Angel, to the feline family. Once a hobo, the largest of the cats is 30-pound Toby, "whom people mistake for a dog," says Nelle. She touts the cats as "a fantastic collection of wonderful creatures who never cease to offer unconditional love and loyalty."

Nelle and Aleece's early experience saving cats at a highway-side dumpster left Nelle with sentiments not as bouncy as her feelings for cats. "I have very dark thoughts about people who abandon animals," she said. For two years, the sisters transported their garbage eight miles to a local dump site on U.S. Highway 1 in Georgia. One day they noticed a cat scrounging in the area. During their next stop, the cat sauntered in again.

After several trips to the site, they realized the same cats were there again and again, first one, two, then more. Nelle began counting the many who emerged. In varying pedigrees, ranging from one Himalayan to a scruffy calico mix, twelve cats were tallied. The feral mix had staked the dumpster as a food source.

After further exploring the surrounding area, Aleece and Nelle realized the cats took refuge in the remains of a burned-down church building, a long ago chapel where Nelle's great-grandfather once pastored. They grew troubled thinking about the cats scrambling through dumpsters of waste and living in a collapsed building of charred timber.

"We have to do the most we can," said Aleece. It became a routine to load the car with a sack of generic cat food after lifting their bags of garbage into the trunk. They began setting out bowls of water and food near the dumpsters. The wild cats looked terrified, eyes fixed upon them with fierce hostility. But regular feedings solicited the beginning of trust. The starved cats

soon learned to recognize the sound of the car motor and ran out of the weeds toward the dumpsters before Aleece stopped the engine. They remained skittish but were hungry enough to overcome their apprehension.

"Before long, we got attached to the motley bunch and called the Humane Society. We asked if they would help us capture the cats and move them to a place of safety. Because the animals were outside the city limits, the organization was not allowed to assist," Nelle said. "Aleece insisted that we come up with a solution, so we scratched our heads and decided that a contribution might twist their arm." They called back and promised a donation of five hundred dollars if the staff would aid them in a rescue effort.

The Society agreed and began by putting out humane traps. The first catch netted two chickens and two cats. The chickens were released and the cats were taken to the shelter. Unborn kittens of two pregnant females were spared a life of scavenging. Eventually, most of the cats were trapped.

"Sometime later, the dumpsters were removed," said Nelle, "but that does not solve the problem of people who leave helpless animals to fend for themselves."

Not only deserted cats, but populations of impoverished people indicate there may always be those who are destitute. Even children in many parts of the world must raid garbage dumps for salvageable goods and food. Like Aleece, "we have to do the most we can." The sisters were moved in their hearts and reached deeply into their purses to change a pitiful situation. The combination of compassion and action can change almost anything.

The Tail End

The poor you will always have with you.
Matthew 26:11 NIV

Necessary Intrusions

It was late evening of move-in day at Joe's new apartment in Portland, Oregon. He looked in closets, stooped under beds, scanned every room, checked under tables, and inspected empty boxes. Intermittently he called, "Thai! Thai!" Joe Ryan's long-haired Siamese was missing.

After repeated postponements, the apartment manager had notified Joe to confirm that work was nearly completed at the new complex. At last, he could move in. Thai and Joe had waited seven dull days in a cramped and lonely motel room.

The carpet layers were still hammering and stretching when movers huffed the first large crate through the front door of the apartment. Other contractors wandered in and out as they finished details on the newly-constructed building where Joe and his family would be the first occupants. All afternoon the moving van had spewed boxes and furniture which it had swallowed the previous week.

Movers wrestled the last pieces of furniture and a few boxes up the steep stairway to the loft. A little past dinner hour, the van pulled away and Joe realized he was hungry. He presumed Thai must be also. He called again. "C'mon Thai, let's eat!" Joe was convinced his cat was simply hiding—surely not gone.

He looked again on the ground level, on the balcony and loft. He called, first softly and then loudly. "At appropriate times," Joe said, "Thai's name becomes two syllables, 'Ty-ee.' I raise my voice on the first syllable and lower it on the second." But even Joe's affectionate intonation failed to route the cat.

Though frustrated, his unsuccessful search for Thai had not overly disturbed him. He had watched the doors, knew the windows were closed, and therefore, he suspected Thai was safely ensconced somewhere, waiting for strangers to leave. But underlying doubt gnawed at him.

Anger too began adding to the weariness of the day. *Cats are ungrateful,* Joe mused. *For three years I've spent big bucks on vet bills and cat food, transported this cat hundreds of miles to our new locale, and what do I get? Annoyance!* Possible rebukes from his wife and daughter also filled his imagination, that would surely come if, in fact, the cat *was* lost. He concluded it was better the girls were still in San Diego.

Again he pondered the cat's escape options. The only exit possible had been the front door, and Joe had noticed Thai was too petrified of carpentry noises to have ventured in that direction. Surely Thai would emerge. Joe settled down with a snack and plugged in the portable TV.

Prime-time programming ended—still no Thai. Joe was ready for bed. A sudden thought struck him. He wondered if Thai had walked into one of the two small openings in the loft walls leading into attics of other apartments.

Could he have fallen into an unfinished lower level? Where else could he be? Joe remembered one of the workers sealing the holes.

He tromped upstairs. He called softly and then again loudly. Down on his knees, he tilted his head near the floor where metal wall-plates sealed the tomb of everything below. Not a sound. He moved to the other end of the loft and pressed his ear to the floor. "Ty-ee, are you there?" Not a whine, not a meow.

Joe was nagged by his strong suspicion. He found a screwdriver and loosened the first metal plate. "Ty-ee, Ty-ee," he called into the echoing darkness. Disappointing silence.

Unsatisfied, he sprinted across the loft to the other plate which he pried off and set aside. He bent his head close to the opening. Only six inches away sat Thai, his suddenly mute cat. His placid expression seemed to say he had enjoyed the brief recluse. If nothing else, it was a good game.

"If Thai had been a child, I would've scolded him. 'Why did you do this to me? Why didn't you answer when I called?' But honestly," Joe said, "I felt like chiding myself. 'Why didn't I take better care and leave him for the day with a boarder or a friend?'

"It was enough to know he wouldn't starve and suffer, trapped in an attic hole. It was enough he was found and I could go to bed without worry. That one rare night, Thai shared my warm bed. If there's ever another move, my wife or daughter will accompany me, not my elusive cat."

Thankfully, Joe sought out his cat even though Thai indicated no desire for help. Thai's hideaway seemed to him like a sensible place of protection. But Joe's perception was more realistic. Trapped, Thai would die unless he was found and delivered.

Sometimes it seems that God intrudes upon human affairs. He suddenly appears and unsettles our environs. We are offended by the intrusion of undesirable circumstances. But God's greater knowledge gives Him a view like Joe's. He realizes we are in danger unless He frees us. The next time it looks like God is "horning in," trust Him. You've probably just been rescued though unaware you were even in peril.

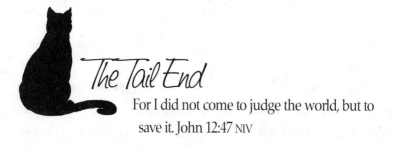

The Tail End

For I did not come to judge the world, but to save it. John 12:47 NIV

Biker Cat

Rastus loved the wind in his whiskers. The sixteen-pound cat was born in Vancouver, Canada, and rode over 300,000 kilometers on motorcycles with Max Corkill, animal activist and fund-raiser. The cat's favorite stance was with front paws on the headlight, rear paws on the petrol tank, and tail in the air, while chugging along at 25 kmh. Both were equipped with helmets, one of them, custom-made. The adventuresome pair was a novel sight.

The unlikely twosome raised thousands of dollars of support for SPCA branches in tours throughout New Zealand. Rastus had his own fan club with T-shirts and polos, buttons, and photos which sported several poses of the precocious cat. Proceeds from collectibles were donated to various SPCA's to assist less fortunate animals.

Many cats have gained notoriety for trick performances and for product endorsements, but few have earned the spotlight as charity stars. Rastus had his own bank account and wrote many checks—signed with his paw—for the welfare of animals.

Corkill had found the abandoned kitten at a biker's swap meet in Canada. The two were a match. Max and Rastus went everywhere together, including restaurants. Only once were they refused entrance. When Max walked out holding Rastus, customers followed. They were more interested in seeing the famous cat than in eating.

Everyone wanted to pet Rastus. Normally, the cat was tolerant, but when he grew weary with attention, he expressed it with an odd growl. Fortunately, Max had a way of handling touchy situations with diplomacy. One day at a showground, a little girl ignored Max's warning not to touch the cat, and she provoked a wee bite, soon made better by receiving a free picture signed by Rastus. In characteristic tact, Max promised to send the little girl a special badge which read, "I've been bitten by Rastus."

The biker cat drank filtered water and ate select food. Nothing but the best for this active cat. "Rastus performed like a trained dog," said Cherie Bromley of Nelson RSPCA, "sitting, staying, and eating on command, well, most of the time." Like all cats, the nine-year-old Bombay-cross had a mind of his own. Corkill told Ms. Bromley that Rastus loved the speed of the motorbike. As a kitten, he used to sleep on the bike, and he would jump on of his own accord when Corkill cranked the engines. Max sometimes wore a badge that read, "Max Corkill, Chauffeur for Rastus."

Max and his black cat were last seen by the Nelson, New Zealand, SPCA shelter in November 1997. Only two months later, Rastus, Max, and his pillion passenger, Ms. Gaynor Martin, were killed in a head-on collision in North Taranaki, New Zealand. Corkill, aged fifty-eight, had been a member of several motorcycle clubs and was reputed as a notably safe cycler. The driver of the car that crashed into them was at fault in the accident.

At a Memorial Service conducted at St. Peter's Church in Nelson, Corkill and Martin were described as, " . . . genuinely warm, friendly and good-humored; you felt like you'd known them for years."

The celebrity threesome will always be remembered by the Nelson SPCA—Max on his Sunbeam motorbike, Rastus with his front paws on the headlight, bandana whipping in the wind, and "mum" seated behind.

The tragic deaths of Rastus, Max and Gaynor cannot diminish the impact of their service to the animal organizations they supported. Perhaps it is better to live a shortened life well, than to live a long life without meaning—especially if you have as much fun as the respected biker trio, Max, Gaynor, and Rastus, the Easy Rider cat.[10]

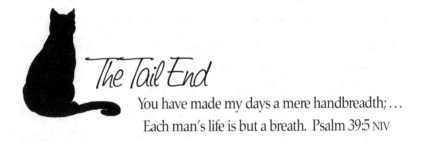

The Tail End

You have made my days a mere handbreadth; . . .
Each man's life is but a breath. Psalm 39:5 NIV

Pur-r-rsistence Pays Off

$\mathcal{S}$anta Claus's legendary descent down the chimney is similar to a feline rendition told by Dr. and Mrs. John Moyer of Spokane, Washington. John, a retired physician and his wife, Joanne, own an extraordinary Craftsman home on Spokane's South Hill. Built in 1906, the stately nine-room mansion sits among Northwest firs, pines, and maples, and has earned a listing in the National Registry of Historic Places.

Just three steps inside the front door, visitors view refinished oak floors, antique brass hardware, egg and dart molding, and quarter-sawn oak woodwork. Previously, the home was the twenty-year residence of newspaper editor, Henry Rising. The house is both magnificent and inviting. A select few of the family cats stroll amid period furniture and pad across oriental rugs, seemingly indifferent to their grand abode.

Long-haired calico Katie introduced herself to the Moyers on their front veranda during a political fund-raiser they hosted. For each kind stroke that campaigners offered Katie, she exchanged a sprinkle of fleas. The next day

Joanne had her bathed, wormed, and medicated for ear mites. Katie had found a home.

Black and orange speckled Molly would have died had the Moyers not adopted her and sought treatment for a serious infection stemming from a septic abortion. Molly holds the honor of being the primary indoor cat.

Siamese Sandy kept arriving for meals until Joanne attached a note to his collar. "This cat is always hungry. If he has an owner, call me." An unidentified caller replied, but Sandy kept returning. The day Joanne found him on the porch with a compound fracture from a probable brush with a car, she rushed him to the vet. Sandy recovered and has stayed. The anonymous owner has never inquired.

Motley, a tawny tabby, was originally owned by Dr. Moyer's daughter. But Motley preferred the doctor's company over brotherhood with the large dogs that carried him around in their mouths at the daughter's home.

And Ginger, an amalgam of canine breeds, would likely feel slighted if she was not named. The four cats and one dog shared the home until the December advent of yet another pet.

One festive evening near Christmas, the Moyers entertained guests in the gracious Great Room. Joanne poured holiday blend coffee, and conversed, though somewhat distracted by the whimper of a cat. The meow was muffled and unfamiliar. After the visitors left, Joanne said flatly. "I hear a cat crying, John, and it's not one of ours." She listened in the now quiet room and then pointed. "It's coming from the fireplace."

Together they squatted on the tile hearth. A mild but distressed cry was heard again. Dr. Moyer set aside the fire screen, removed the grate and maneuvered his upper body into the black recess. Gazing up into the dark

flue he saw two golden eyes of a coal-black cat peeking over the edge of the partially opened damper, which was jammed by leaves. The doctor grabbed the cat's head with his free hand, while clasping the damper handle lest it close around the cat's neck. The comical drama could not have occurred in a more glorious setting. A handsome oil portrait of the doctor hung on the floral-papered wall above him, as he lay on his back, gripping cat and damper.

He called to Joanne who stood watching the curious venture. "Bring me a chunk of wood so I can shove open the damper and get hold of him with both hands." Joanne quickly returned with a block from the basement. With the damper fully opened, the cat fell to Dr. Moyer's chest in a puff of soot. The panicked animal wiggled from his hands, but Joanne caught him before he made a trail of ashen footprints across the carpet.

Joanne recognized him immediately as the half-grown cat with the red collar she had noticed while spading in the garden. Once before he had entered her house through a heat duct when a neighbor was cat-sitting. At another time, the cat had meowed atop the roof and Joanne had pulled him through a third floor window. He seemed intent on joining the family, but Joanne was equally intent on sending him home.

That December night the intruding cat's novel entrance demanded a decision. Joanne towel-wiped some of the soot from his fur and temporarily put him downstairs where all the cats had a bed. "We've got him, now what are we going to do with him?" she asked John. They decided to keep him. Joanne brought him back upstairs, bathed him, and dried his glossy black coat.

When John began calling him Chimney, a most apropos name, it was clear that cat number five had been added to the family. "Chimmy" was the

first Christmas present of the season and he had arrived in Scandinavian style—down the chimney—though without a bag of toys.

When Chimmy dropped the three stories to the damper shelf that night, perhaps it was a last resort to secure adoption. Mrs. Moyer had ignored him while she gardened. Nor had he succeeded in winning his welcome when he pushed open the heat register. And each time he was removed from the roof, he was again placed outside. Chimmy's awkward and abrupt entrance down the chimney had at last won him acceptance. He finally earned his welcome, though Chimmy might say, "It was a little slow in being extended."

Persistence paid off for Chimmy. A variety of efforts, methods, and appeals were necessary. But those who know what they are after will persist until they achieve their ends.

The Tail End

When you meet with resistance, face it with persistence.

Miracles Close By

In addition to raising eight children, Clara Hall tended a large garden, canned its harvest, churned butter, cooked meals, and washed the clothes of ten people. Life presented such a variety of challenges, at times Clara supposed she could do almost anything that fell into her lap. Years later, she discovered it was literally true.

Clara and Eli lived with their children on a dairy farm in Missouri. Paul, David, Jimmy, Edith, Alice, Naomi, Noreen, and Ruth did their share of the farm chores to help their father, who was employed full-time at the nearby milk plant.

Clara believed in keeping cats to rid their property of mice. In her estimation, cats were as important as cows, chickens, and rabbits. She spoiled the cats on fresh milk which she insisted the children give to them after each milking, morning and night.

When, one by one, the children reached adulthood and left home, Clara's busy life began to ebb. One daughter went to the mission field, others married, and some moved West to find better jobs. After the children left, Eli sold most of the cows. But Clara was attached to her cats and kept them all.

The cats became companions who helped her adjust to the empty house that had previously simmered with activity. Clara talked to the cats like she used to banter with the children.

The cats seemed to realize they had been elevated to a higher echelon at the farm. Instead of roaming through the barn and tagging behind children, now they played and slept near the house. Anytime Clara went outdoors, she had to shoo sleepy cats off the steps lest she trip. They returned her "skeddadle" with affectionate rubs against her billowy skirt as she strolled to the roadside mailbox. When she weeded the garden, cats peeked behind lettuce heads and jumped between onion shoots. As Clara collected the eggs, cats accompanied her. They chased the hens and sent them squawking and fluttering in fright. The void in Clara's heart from her empty nest was filled by a family of felines.

One kitty she called Mommy Cat had supplied the farm with lots of frisky mousers through the years. Mommy was Clara's favored pet. One afternoon, Clara noticed Mommy's tummy was swelling with new life. She found a box and prepared a cushy bed for the coming kittens.

Several days later, Clara settled her weary body into the rocking chair. As was her habit, she fitted smudged bifocals across her nose and opened a well-worn Bible in her lap. She prayed for her adult children and trusted God's peace-giving words. Clara was always diligent to protect those sacred moments from interruption. But her efforts to wait upon God were disturbed that day.

Just then, Mommy Cat made a silent leap into Clara's lap, paws treading on Holy Writ, and whiskers tickling Clara's arm. "Get down, Mommy Cat!" Clara brushed her aside, but Mommy remained close by.

Clara tried again to concentrate on promises of Scripture. But Mommy intruded upon the serene moment once more. She jumped into Clara's lap and was swiftly pushed off. A third time, Mommy approached the rocker, locked upon Clara's gaze, and moved her mouth in a soundless meow.

At last, the insistent kitty persuaded Clara, who invited Mommy to join her sanctum. Clara laid her Bible on the table and tapped her leg signaling Mommy to her lap. "C'mon up, if you must." Mommy answered with a thankful meow.

"You're gonna have them kittens soon," said Clara, as she glided her hand over the cat's full belly. Mommy commenced to purr. Clara rested her head against the maple spines of the rocker and soon both owner and kitty were asleep.

Clara dozed until she was awakened to the movement of cat feet making circles on her thighs. With eyes still closed, Clara stroked Mommy and stole another reprieve of midday slumber.

In a frustrated attempt to get comfortable, Mommy rearranged her body, waking Clara again. "Mommy, you settle down! You disturbed my prayer time and now you're robbin' me of a nap," Clara scolded. She tried to ignore the restless cat and slipped back to sleep.

When Clara awoke, she felt a warm moisture through her skirt, and her half-open eyes beheld two newborn kittens in her lap. The birth of another was in progress. Having borne eight infants herself, Clara respected the wonder of the event and sat still until the last kitten was delivered.

Clara was suddenly remorseful for chiding Mommy and shoving her to the floor. "I've lived a long time and done a lot of things," she said, "but I never thought my lap would serve as delivery table for a cat."

As Clara spent moments of devotion in her rocker that day, little did she realize what God had in mind. While she rocked and slept, Clara had served God and nature, practically as well as prayerfully. Many of God's assignments are obvious. They present themselves in our lap. Perhaps God is most pleased when we faithfully attend to duties closest by. When we do, miracles occur right before our eyes.

The Tail End

What lands in our lap may have
been tossed there by God.

147

Cash and a Cat

On a freezing winter afternoon in Brooklyn, New York, Paul Franzetti jogged to the automated bank machine. His motive for running was financial, not physical. A dead car battery had mandated a need for quick cash.

Paul and his wife Maria had been forced to take public transportation to work earlier that morning. Paul promised Maria he would buy a new battery after work. Wanting to avoid an unnecessary purchase, Maria urged him to call their road assistance service. "But Paul is as headstrong as I am cheap," said Maria, "so he won in the debate about servicing or buying. As I braced my cold body for the walk to the bus stop, the certainty of reliable transportation suddenly felt worth the investment."

When Paul got home from the bank that afternoon, he tried to start the engine. Dead as a mummy. A neighbor, Tony, noticed Paul tinkering under the hood and came to help. Long after Paul gave up on the battery, Tony persisted—he wiggled cables, cleaned connections, and finally got it started.

Paul jumped inside and headed for the subway to pick up Maria, who presumed the car was equipped with the new battery. Thus she was curious when Paul passed by their home. "I guess you're wondering where we're going," he teased.

Maria gulped. Was there something worse wrong with the car? She hoped for the best. "Okay," she speculated, "we're going to the gas station to have the battery charged; you want to make sure it's in top condition." She played along.

"Not quite." Bypassing their home in no way related to car troubles; it related entirely to a cat.

"There was a kitten at the cash machine," he explained. "I promised God I would go back for it if I didn't have to buy a new battery. I knew you'd like the part about not having to buy a battery, but what do you think about the part concerning a cat?"

What a loaded question! Maria hesitated.

"Well Maria, that's the story. Are we gonna keep my deal with God?"

Now Maria was faced with a decision about breaking a promise to God and deserting a kitten. *Not fair,* she thought. *Who in their sane mind could say no!* But, they already had two cats.

"Well, let's go before it freezes to death!" Maria's heart was now engaged. "I secretly told myself that one more cat was no big deal."

Paul smiled. Approval from the wife adds joy to everything!

They pulled alongside the curb at the bank machine and noticed the forlorn animal look pleadingly into the eyes of a man completing his transaction. Maria jumped out and reached for the kitten who dug tiny claws into her coat. The outline of ribs was visible through mottled, grimy fur.

Once in the car, the kitten clung so tightly, Maria had to pry her claws free to buckle the seat belt.

"We've got to have her tested before she's around our other cats," Maria insisted. Paul agreed and though the vet clinic was ready to close, the doctor knew them and opened the door. By now, Maria wanted the kitten and prayed she would test negative for diseases.

The vet estimated the kitten had been fending alone for at least two months. "I shudder to think about any animal enduring sub-zero temperatures that long," said Maria. The kitten's ears were bare of fur from rubbing them in the intense cold.

What a relief when the test results were negative. But to Maria's chagrin, the vet bills were costlier than the price of a battery! "But," she consoled herself, "we kept a promise to God! Wasn't that more important than a few extra dollars?"

That night Maria put the pitiful feline in a spare bedroom with water, food, and litter. The kitten cowered under the bed for awhile, but finally stepped out, and headed straight for the water bowl. She drank and drank and drank. "A surge of pity welled up inside me for stray animals who need water." Maria put the kitten under a comforter where she lay with head on her paws. She was too weak to respond cheerily to the comforts and sustenance now available—too weak to do anything but let recovery begin.

"Twice in the night I checked on her, half afraid I would find her dead," said Maria. "She must have been incredibly relieved to be warm and fed."

"During the next few days I noticed something peculiar. She didn't meow, groom or purr. But soon I saw changes. First, she found her appetite. Then one afternoon I set her beside me on the couch and she gave her paw one swift lick. Several hours later she began to groom and didn't stop for nearly an hour. And at last came the reward of her purr."

Paul and Maria made a few weak attempts to find a home, but in their hearts they both knew "Apples" was theirs.

"Of our three cats, Apples is the most attached to us and reciprocates our rescue with lots of love," said Maria.

Does God strike bargains? When Paul promised he would return for the cat if the battery started, it was a game he was playing with himself. If God could be manipulated, He would not be God. Our prayers move the heart of God, but they do not shove Him into a corner. Promises we make when we want God to return a favor, are really the decisions we know we should make anyway. "If you help me pass this test, I'll join the church choir." God's leading can always be trusted to be the best choice. The stuff of, "If You will, I will," is a game we should avoid.

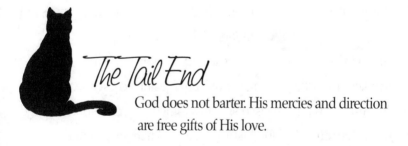

The Tail End

God does not barter. His mercies and direction are free gifts of His love.

The Ties That Bind

*T*wo black kittens with emerald green eyes stood shivering on Nancy Wilcox's patio in Little Rock, Arkansas, on a chilly November day in 1990. The brother-sister duo were obviously frightened. Incapable of closing the door on the pitiful creatures, Nancy took them in. "I guess they kind of warmed my heart," she admitted. Nancy soon confirmed that the abandoned kittens did not belong to any of her neighbors. "They were so pretty, I couldn't understand why someone would have dumped them," she said.

Nancy kept the kittens separated from her jealous cocker spaniel who had no interest in hosting the visitors. A towel-lined box set outdoors served as a warm and adequate bed for the furry guests. While Nancy pondered the future of the kittens, she observed their personalities. Though siblings, their temperaments were quite different. The male, with the distinctive white paws, acted the part of a protective brother, draping himself over his sleeping sister each night. But during the day his self-interests were prevalent. "He kept trying to eat his sister's food," said Wilcox. "He was always the aggressive one."

Nancy made earnest attempts to find permanent homes for the kittens. Her best help came from Anita, a neighbor who was a piano teacher. Nancy was going out of town for the weekend and asked if she could leave the kittens with Anita and put a "Free Kittens" sign on her door. Neither Anita nor Nancy could have guessed the fate and fame which lay ahead for one of the kittens.

The Arkansas governor's wife, Hillary Clinton, brought her then ten-year-old daughter Chelsea for a scheduled piano lesson at Anita's home. Two black kittens listened to the music while eyeing Mrs. Clinton. Chelsea was still mourning the loss of her cocker spaniel, who had recently died in a car accident. "Both Mrs. Clinton and Chelsea were raving about the cute little cats," said Anita. "Hillary asked for the little guy with the white toes." In one short hour, white-toed Socks had gained a home, received a name, and even had a piano lesson. Socks was headed to the governor's mansion while his sister was left behind.

This second abandonment was probably harder on the sister kitten than the first desertion by the original owners. "She looked pitiful," said Nancy. Compassion for the remaining kitten pressed Nancy to locate a loving home. She dressed the feline in a fashionable red and green Gucci bow and visited her best friend Carolyn Hartstein, whose dog had recently died. Carolyn's granddaughter secured the future of kitten number two. "Courtny took one look and fell in love," said Carolyn. Midnight had a name and a new home.

Now both kittens enjoy a life of pampered luxury. Socks, a true aristo-cat, trips about the White House grounds and poses for portraits. Midnight n'er complains about her less prominent lifestyle lounging on soft pillows, nibbling on canned salmon and chicken, and viewing squirrels through the windows.

The biggest difference between the brother and sister cats is their paw-litical pur-r-rsuasions. Midnight's mistress is a Republican. Carolyn said, "We tell Midnight, 'You could have been in the White House now, and Socks could have been here with us.'" Midnight feels neither inferior to nor envious of her Democratic sibling. Midnight's attitude is, "So what? Socks is still my brother."

On the long list of things that divide people is politics. To hold differing views about government, issues, and beliefs is what makes a country free. To love a brother or sister in spite of conflicting opinions is what demonstrates godly character and makes a nation strong. Don't let politics divide kinships.

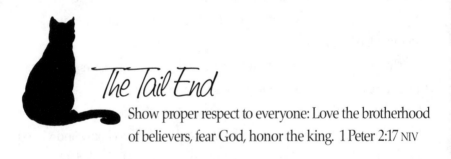

The Tail End

Show proper respect to everyone: Love the brotherhood of believers, fear God, honor the king. 1 Peter 2:17 NIV

Beyond Understanding

On November 18, 1996, a freezing storm dropped over an inch of ice on the Inland Northwest. By evening the next day, Ice Storm '96 left 250,000 people shivering in the area's worst storm-related disaster in 100 years.

Within hours, fundamental conveniences in 100,000 homes were cut off—water heaters, furnaces, electric lighting, telephone service, and electrically powered televisions and radios. Chilled hands reached for car keys as residents headed for grocery stores to stock up on nonperishable food, candles, batteries, flashlights, and battery-powered radios.

Within fourteen days, electricity was restored to most homes, though hundreds remained without power for longer periods. Many stayed with relatives, neighbors, or at community shelters established to handle the state of emergency.

Ellie Lee and her three cats were among the many residents without electricity. For three days they camped indoors. Ellie swaddled herself in blankets wrapped over layers of clothing. Viewing the vapor of her breath

inside her home was an unwelcome novelty. "Women at the grocery store were dressed for ski slopes," said Ellie. Earmuffs, gloves, and heavy shoes fortified them for shopping in unheated supermarkets where thawing freezer foods were reduced for quick sale.

Ice-laden tree limbs damaged lateral power lines. Toppled trees impaled cars and snapped wires blocked driveways and streets. One heroic technician was killed as he attempted repairs. There were other griefs, though unequal. A newspaper correspondent watched her husband bemoan a fallen tree in their backyard. Its age rings numbered 114.

But the human spirit triumphed in the icy face of struggle. A church placard read, "No church services this weekend. Pray for power!" Spray painted on a piece of plywood were the words, "Will work for electricity."

The enduring, relentless cold is what most people recall about Ice Storm '96. As powerless days continued, generators also sold out. Parents battled the indoor chill by keeping their children near fireplaces that roared with the coveted warmth. Even pets, like Ellie's cats, were intolerant of the cold— Harold in particular.

The big orange cat with one eyelid stitched closed, (his missing eye was a loss blamed on glaucoma) had announced his intentions to live with Ellie two years earlier by settling himself at her back door. He knew he belonged there and waited for Ellie to catch on. When it was plain that Harold had no home, Ellie invited him to stay.

No longer a transient, Harold and his two cat companions depended on the regularity of oil heat in the winter and the reprieve of cool basement floors during summer. Of the three, Harold was the "heat freak." Perhaps bygone days as a stray had etched in his memory the misery of winter nights huddled near chimneys or in frigid garages, only to be banished by strangers in the morning. Some cats have a penchant for pillows, some crave tuna. But Harold had a thing for warmth.

On that November day, when the temperature in the house suddenly dropped to levels Harold recalled only from the years of his outdoor life, he began following Ellie, keeping his one golden eye fixed upon her. Since Ellie was doing nothing about the conditions, Harold decided he had better try something.

Dangling from Ellie's heat registers were two-inch chains for opening and closing the heat ducts. When the furnace came on, forced air rattled the chains as they chinked against the metal registers. After the first blast of air, the chains hung still.

That first bitter night, Ellie awoke to a noise in her bedroom. She sat up and there was Harold, pawing the chain. Ellie realized this was not simply cold weather entertainment for a bored cat. Prior to the ice storm, Harold had never played with the chains.

Ellie spoke to him. "Harold, you're a pretty clever guy, but that won't help. When the heat comes on, the chain rattles, but rattling the chain won't bring the heat." Harold was not persuaded. Ellie called him back to bed but he continued his attempt to prompt the sequence—chain rattles, warm air follows. Frustrated, he jumped on the bed and nudged his big head under the covers. A few hours later, he woke Ellie again, rattling the chain. For the next three days, Harold swatted the chains in a futile effort to ignite the furnace.

Harold was as glad as thousands of others in the vicinity when restored power allowed furnaces to hum and chains to jingle. Once again, the comfort of warm air blew against the orange fur of the cat with the deductive mind. Smart as he was, poor Harold probably never did understand why his chain rattling took so long to instigate the flow of warm air.

Some things in life do not make sense. Harold thought he understood the heat sequence, but failed when he tried to make it work. Though God gave us extraordinary minds, at times His operations do not follow lines of human rationale. It is then that He asks us to trust. Unfortunately, "trust Me" periods of life are often cold seasons—seasons we wish we could skip, seasons like Ice Storm '96 that we are glad to see pass. Though trust may seem contrary to logic, trust in God is the most sensible foundation for reason.[11]

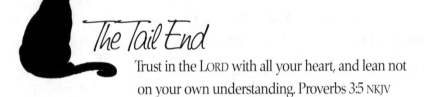

The Tail End

Trust in the LORD with all your heart, and lean not on your own understanding. Proverbs 3:5 NKJV

Add a Little Sugar

When Lisa Huskey brought home a curly poodle with soft brown fur, her children were elated. The next morning, Stephanie sprinkled brown sugar on her oatmeal and exclaimed, "Mommy, let's name the doggie Sugar!" It was settled when Justin stammered in his two-year-old simplicity, "I like Sugar."

Soon after, the Huskey family bred Sugar to a handsome stud, and she gave birth to two adorable puppies. Sugar was a doting mother. After her young were adopted, she searched for them and whimpered for days.

Being the matriarch she was, perhaps she may have been eager for another litter of puppies to care for. But this time she chose her own beau. Sugar lived outdoors, so she had many attentive suitors.

Soon a litter of mongrels was born in the backyard. The colorful assortment of solid and patchwork offspring delighted the mother's heart once again.

Twice more Sugar mated and delivered a hodgepodge of pups. The Huskeys were weary with finding homes for her babies, so they had her spayed. But Sugar lost her vitality when she was no longer bearing, nursing, and licking puppies. The Huskeys suspected she was lonely.

Following the birth of another son, Ryan, the family moved to Missouri. Bob, the minister-father, became pastor to a parish in Neosho. The parsonage was located on the church campgrounds. An ever-increasing number of stray animals on the grounds prompted Bob to suggest they rename the camp, Animal Kingdom.

One afternoon as Lisa was preparing supper, she heard a tiny "mew." She looked outside but saw no cats. She returned to peel potatoes and heard a triad of cries. "Mew, mew, mew."

Just then Bob came in and heard the kitten, too. Asking no one in particular, he said, "Who's brought a cat into this house? Cats belong outdoors." He remembered his sister's allergy to cats and worried that maybe he and his children had inherited the same intolerance.

"Did you hear that, Lisa? There's a cat in here," Bob affirmed.

"Where is that kitten?" Lisa was puzzled herself.

The feline complaint was uttered again. "Mee-ewww."

"I think it's coming from behind the stove," Lisa said. Bob pulled the range away from the wall and out jumped a white kitten with gray tail and paws.

Bob was not pleased.

"Probably another campground drop-off," Lisa suggested.

By then their two boys and Sugar the dog had come to investigate the mysterious visitor in the kitchen. Bob picked up the kitten by the nape of its neck. Holding it toward the boys, he said, "Justin, did you bring this kitten inside?"

"Nope," he answered.

"Ryan, how about you?"

"Not me," young Ryan answered.

Stephanie joined the commotion in the kitchen. "How about you, Steph, did you bring the kitten inside?"

"No Daddy, I promise, I didn't. I've never seen that kitten on the campgrounds."

But then Sugar gave herself away. She stood up on her short hind legs and reached for the kitten. With her front paws on Bob's pants, she tiptoed on her rear feet and danced her curiosity.

"Look Dad, Sugar wants to see!" Ryan reached for the kitten and set it on the floor. Sugar immediately licked the kitten who snuggled as close to her as possible.

Now Sugar was on the hot seat. Bob addressed the dog. "Sugar, did you pack that kitten in the house?" Sugar lifted her head toward Bob and fixed her chocolate eyes upon him. Bob read her reply.

"I sure did. This kitten needs a home and I need a baby," was Bob's interpretation of Sugar's rapt interest.

For all Bob's gruff interrogation of the family, he made a quick and favorable decision in the dog's behalf. "Well Sugar, I guess you're in charge of the cat. You can keep your baby as long as it's outside." Bob lifted the small pair, one in each arm, and set them on the porch.

Lisa filled a saucer with warm milk and placed it before the kitten. Kitty buried her nose in the milk, then pulled away coughing and sneezing. She had probably never drunk from a bowl. But the hungry kitten was not dissuaded. Kitty tried again, then coughed and sneezed once more. At this point, Sugar intervened. She took a few laps of milk and stepped back. The kitten caught on after one lesson. This time Kitty lapped, but held her nose above the milk. Sugar had accepted her responsibility and seemed delighted to have someone to nurture.

That night the kitten slept against Sugar's belly in the dog bed. The next morning Justin found the kitten suckling on Sugar. Though Sugar was not producing milk, the kitten was satisfied with a live pacifier. As Kitty suckled, Sugar licked her from ears to tail tip.

No one reacted with allergy symptoms, and all the family turned out to be pleased with "what the dog drug in." Bob decided that his calling to share salvation with the populace in Neosho included the rescue of a white and gray kitten.

As for Sugar, she knew what she needed and she sought after it. Amidst the busyness of careers and commitments, we sometimes fail to pursue the simple pleasures we know will make us happy. People who enjoy life are those who satisfy their legitimate desires, even if the wish is as simple as reading a good book thirty minutes each day. Clarifying our needs and granting them will add a lot of sugar to our lives.

The Tail End

Near the end of their lives, people often regret having denied themselves the simple things that were attainable.

Acting It Out

In 1986, when Bob the Weather Cat first appeared on videotape one Friday night on TV station KATU in Portland, Oregon, the public response was overwhelming. Encores, encores, and more encores were requested for the feline sensation.

The wife of station news photographer, Bob Foster, found the gray and white stray cat in the neighborhood. After that first TV appearance, weatherman Jeff Gianola held up a pair of doll-size sunglasses and said to Foster, "Put these on that cat of yours. It'll be great!" Jeff's impulse was the beginning of the cat's signature costumes. On the tape that followed, the Weather Cat was dressed to match the forecast. Fan mail confirmed the instant popularity of the cat whom Gianola named Bob.

For several years, the garbed cat wowed viewers wearing clothing that suited the weather forecast or typified the nearest holiday. At Christmastime he wore a Santa suit, and on St. Patrick's day he dressed like a leprechaun. Area seamstresses, young and old, volunteered their talents to tailor the outfits. In warm weather he wore shorts and tank tops, with sunglasses of course, and in cold weather he donned scarves and earmuffs. He was even attired in a tutu and little ballet slippers when the Russian Bolshoi Ballet performed in Portland.

One night the producers were reluctant to follow the tragic evening news concerning The Gulf War with the cat's capers, so the show aired without him. Viewers instantly expressed their disappointment. The switchboard lit up with callers inquiring about Bob, the Weather Cat. The station concluded that people needed the whimsical appearance of the cat to help balance grim news.

"When Bob died of cancer, it was a day of mourning in the city," said Foster. "Phone callers offered condolences, some sent flowers, and elderly ladies who had watched the cat for over seven years called weeping." Many grieved the loss of the feline celebrity.

Soon after, Foster promoted Bob's roommate, Tom(cat), to step into Bob's shoes—literally. Tom, who had long watched Bob from the sidelines, now appeared on TV wearing boots for rainy weather forecasts and other apparel that matched the changing climate. Tom's popularity was equal to his predecessor's. Tom even made a few promotional appearances at shopping malls, fairs, school classrooms, and humane society fund-raisers, delighting everyone, cat lovers in pur-r-rticular.

After charming audiences for three and a half years with his weather-ready garments, Tom retired. Like many good things that come to an end, the continued staging of the weather cats was curtailed by an upper-level management decision. But Tom's and Bob's raiment had warmed hearts on

cold days, and cooled tempers on hot ones. They entertained the public with their unique feline appeal.

Tom is no longer fitted into hats, beards, head dresses or uniforms, nor made to endure lights, cameras, and public performances. His days are filled with napping, eating, and playing with other pets and the family children. Tom is as well-loved by his family as by any of his ardent fans. Foster maintains that both the weather cats were first and always special family members.

Unlike a television performance lasting only as long as a 60-second weather forecast, real life calls for the day-in, day-out productions that few viewers see. Even for Bob and Tom, the better parts of their lives were off-stage shows. In real life, we do not merely dress for a part, we must act it out in dramas of struggle and triumph. As someone has said so well, life is not a dress rehearsal. Indeed, it is each person's daily enactment of his or her God-ordained role.

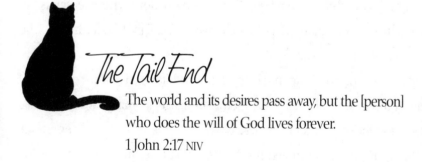

The Tail End

The world and its desires pass away, but the [person] who does the will of God lives forever.
1 John 2:17 NIV

Legacy of a New York Dowager

*P*eople are seldom indifferent to cats. Either they love them or loathe them. Thus, for a cat-loving woman to marry a man who cared nothing for cats, is a bit surprising. A case in point is the story of Kate Mason. The Illinois-born socialite was a beautiful and mysterious woman, who bequeathed more than riches to future generations. The wealthy widow, whose legacy is her love of felines, was married to the rich divorcé, William Hofstra, a man who purportedly disliked cats.

The two married late in life and had no children. Their independence and combined wealth allowed them to engage in many activities. Kate Hofstra's fancies included a variety of animals. She was a noted equestrian. But her love of cats occupied much of her volunteer time. Apparently, Mr. Hofstra's love of Kate surpassed his intolerance for cats. Their mutual interests included travels at home and abroad, the Monday night opera at the Met, and evenings entertaining friends at the Sherry-Netherlands Hotel.

Kate and William lived in a glorious fifteen-acre estate, bordered by a tree-lined thoroughfare, in Hempstead, New York. William's groundsmen landscaped the estate as an arboretum. Their elegant country home was called "The Netherlands" in reference to William's Dutch ancestry, and was not without a special shelter for Kate's cherished Persian, Siamese, and Angora cats. In addition to the horses' stables was a steam-heated structure for the cats behind the rose garden.

Mrs. Hofstra was president of the Atlantic Cat Club. In the Siamese cat division, she won every prize at the cat show in Madison Square Garden, including the Challenge Cup in 1929.

For thirty years, she was vice-president of the Bide-a-wee Home Association in New York City, an organization for the welfare of stray cats. At the time of her death in 1933, she owned twenty-five cats, four dogs, and three parrots.

When William died in May 1932, Kate followed him in death only sixteen months later. She stipulated in her will that the bulk of their estate be established for charitable or public use in memory of her husband.

One fall day in 1934, Howard Brower, executor of the Hofstra estate, rode the Long Island Railroad, seated beside Truesdel Calkins, superintendent of Public Schools in the Village of Hempstead. The two discussed the future of the Hofstra estate. Several days later, Mr. Calkins invited Brower to dinner where he proposed the idea of using the Hofstra facility as a center for higher education. They initiated action that led to the creation of Hofstra College. Just two years after Kate's passing the college doors opened. By 1963, the college had matured into a university.

Mrs. Hofstra's will also allocated ten thousand dollars to the Bide-a-wee association and designated money for the care of all her pets. Her housekeeper, Elizabeth Hiserodt, was willed funds to build a home for herself and given a stipend for maintaining the pets. Until Elizabeth's house was constructed, Kate had provided for her to remain at the family estate with the animals, "so that my pets may continue to be in the same environment to which they are accustomed until the establishment of the home which I have provided . . . where she (Elizabeth) can properly take care of them in substantially the same manner as at present." This was the tender legacy of a New York dowager.

Mrs. Hofstra's sympathies for cats, no doubt, is the basis for a folk tale about Hofstra University. Some believe that stray cats are granted CAT-blanche on university property. Archivist, Geri Solomon, says, "People presume we'll find homes for cats left on the grounds." A family friend of the Hofstra's once said that Mrs. Hofstra picked up "plain old alley cats" as well as exotic breeds. "Though we share Mrs. Hofstra's concern for animals, we realize that a university is not the best home for strays," Geri explained with a smile. Nonetheless, tough-looking tomcats are known to frequent the school grounds, and boxes of kittens are occasionally left on the porch of a building.

The lives of Kate and William Hofstra witness to the strength of diversity in a marriage. Spouses can pursue different interests, though neither needs to share an equal enthusiasm for what the other fancies. When diversity is encouraged, two people are given the opportunity to leave unique contributions for posterity. William's estate became a university for thousands of students. Kate's affection for cats sustained the Bide-a-wee organization in its efforts to protect and nurture neglected cats. William and Kate were a powerful and influential couple whose lives demonstrated how differences can serve effectively and enduringly for the benefit of future generations.[12]

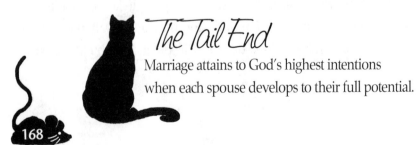

The Tail End

Marriage attains to God's highest intentions when each spouse develops to their full potential.

Expect the Unexpected

$\mathcal{J}$unie was the family poet. She often composed verses about relatives, funny events and memorable times. She loved both her rhymes and her cat, a fifteen-pound Seal Point Siamese named Walter.

Walter and the voices of radio kept Junie company during the day. Tuning in was part of her morning habit. One day a disc jockey announced a contest that caught her attention. "Send in your rhymed jingle promoting Brand Best cat food and you might be the winner of a year's supply of cat food."

Here was a chance to integrate Junie's two loves. She grabbed a pencil and began scribbling ideas that extolled Brand Best. Of course, Walter was no help. He had never eaten prepared cat food as long as Junie had owned him. His diet consisted solely of raw beef heart.

When Junie first adopted Walter years earlier, he had been traumatized and refused to eat. Desperate, she asked her butcher to suggest something that might appeal to the fasting feline. "Beef heart," he recommended. He wrapped up a large heart and wished her luck.

169

Junie hurried home. She diced the meat and dropped a palm-size serving into Walter's dish. She watched with relief as he ate every small chunk and licked the dish. Beef heart became his exclusive diet.

Obviously, anything Junie wrote in the jingle lyrics about Walter's partiality to Brand Best would be fictitious. Irrespective to Walter, she worked hard crafting words for the next few days. She placed the completed poem in the mailbox and waited for the day the winner would be notified.

A letter from the radio station arrived soon after. Junie tore open the envelope. "Thank you for submitting your lyrics. . . . Blah, blah, blah." She skipped to the all-important words in the middle of the page. "You are the winner!" She shook the letter over her head in a self-congratulating gesture. The letter said further that her poem would be broadcast over the air. But the concluding paragraph made her gulp. A cooperating grocery store would host an afternoon appearance of Walter in his cat box eating Brand Best— with a photographer present for pictures!

Junie smiled to herself. She thought the contest was a test of rhyming skills, not a test of her cat's food preference. Off to the supermarket she drove and returned with a can of Brand Best. Though Walter was anticipating his beef heart, she filled his dish with a sampling of the "100 percent nutritious, kidney variety" fare. After one sniff, he expressed his opinion by making burying motions with his paw all around the dish. The ensuing days of offering him Brand Best confirmed that this Siamese was not a flexible feline. After years of beef heart, Walter regarded nothing palatable except his organ meat.

On the day of the store appearance, Junie coaxed Walter into his carrier— no food dish inside. The DJ was waiting for her at the display table. "Congratulations for having written the best lyrics praising Brand Best!" Junie

shook his hand. The photographer slipped an open can of food inside the carrier and waited for a pose. Walter sat coyly in his box, burping his beef heart and ignoring the can. "I fed him at home so he wouldn't be hungry," Junie said, excusing her cat's abstinence.

The competition rules did not require that contestants be cat owners, much less, own a cat who ate Brand Best. The contest was about well-written rhyme, not about the taste preference of the writer's cat. But naturally, everyone, including the photographer, assumed Walter was a connoisseur of Brand Best. Shoppers passed and commented. "Wow, what a big cat. He must like Brand Best." Others tossed sample cans into their carts. After a couple hours, the public attention was over. Though Walter declined even a lick of Brand Best, people loved reading Junie's cute lyrics.

Winning the poetry contest was easier than winning Walter's confidence in canned food. As the free case of food began arriving each month, Junie kept offering it to her finicky fellow. He finally sampled it and decided it was indeed the best brand. At last, Junie's jingle now rang true for even Walter.

Junie made the best of the challenges that came along with her success. And Walter's eventual predilection for the year-long supply of Brand Best created a victory for the cat food budget. The contest event turned out to be win-win for everyone involved.

When Junie's son and daughter were growing up, like all children, they were occasionally faced with the unexpected. Countless times Junie had advised them, "You'll just have to make the best of it." Her experience with Walter and the photographer was a classic opportunity to apply her own counsel. Junie's trophy is more than a memento of her writing ability. It is equally a reminder of how to be unflappable when suddenly surprised by the unexpected.

The Tail End

Nothing is a surprise to God.

Competition Tactics

*C*ompeting for attention with over two dozen felines, some who weigh 600 pounds, can drive a cat to deceit. So it was with Raja, a black and buff long-haired tabby who lives at Cat Tales Zoological Park in Spokane, Washington. Though Raja's domestic species is not endangered, Raja's status was threatened, or so she came to believe.

When Debbie and Mike Wyche, park co-founders, moved to the Northwest, they brought everything they owned, including their four domestic cats. Raja was the eldest of these and had always been top cat.

Soon after settling in north Spokane, the Wyches established Cat Tales. Debbie chose the acrostic which stands for C-are A-bout T-hem, T-ell A-bout the L-ord's E-ndangered S-pecies. The first tours began and ended in the Wyches' home. The gift shop was half of the living room with feline photos posted on the walls. The park tours started at the front door, led down a pathway exhibit, and ended in the kitchen where guests completed questionnaires before exiting out the back door.

Suddenly, Raja was competing for attention with more than just three domestic cats of similar size. The Wyche's affection was now shared with four wild felines in size XXL. The park ended its first summer in 1992 with two tigers, five pumas, a serval, two bobcats, and two lynx. Touring indoors were regular groups of adults and children more interested in the big cats than in Raja. Infant and adolescent cats were always graduated to outdoor habitats, but the indoor enclosures were seldom empty. Newborn tigers and spotted leopards spent weeks of quarantine in the house in sight of the domestics. Raja noticed that Dad Mike and Mom Debbie were increasingly preoccupied with tourists or with care of the large cats.

Raja felt her position at the top of the pet chart was threatened as she witnessed the shift of attention. The wild cats were certainly not family pets, but they deserved and received the Wyches' equal love. Though Raja was still the family's beloved *domestic* cat, she had self-doubts as big as a lion's head.

One day, calamity befell Raja. She broke her front leg in a short fall. When the leg was set in a plaster cast, she soon learned it was useful as a bid for attention. For weeks, she hobbled around, tapping the weighty leg on the linoleum floor, or lugging it along, capitalizing fully on the handicap. She waited for family members to lift her to favorite sleep spots, or waved the straightened leg like Sir Lancelot with his sword. The injury garnered a lot of attention—attention that had slacked noticeably since the *big* cat venture had changed Raja's life.

But Raja healed and x-rays confirmed the bone had mended perfectly. After the cast was removed, Raja demonstrated a slight limp. But even after an adequate period of rehabilitation, Mike and Debbie noticed Raja would occasionally enter a room with a pronounced limp. One day she walked unhindered, and the next day she appeared maimed. Raja's body language did not agree with the veterinarian's x-rays.

Cat Tales, now a nationally recognized zoo and home to dozens of big cats, continues to add members to its family of felines. When the latest big cat took up its temporary residence in the household shelter, the provocation for Raja's limp became plain. The little cat whose gait had been normal, suddenly walked with a gimp. The Wyches caught on when the pattern repeated itself each time something happened at the zoo which spelled competition for Raja. When a newcomer arrived—zoo keeper student, journalist, relative, or a newly rescued cat, Raja performed her crippled act.

Though Mike and Debbie have figured out Raja's ruse, they play along and give her the affection she demands. But Raja thinks everyone is fooled. When media reporters come to interview Mike, Raja comes out limping and solicits an invitation into Mike's lap. If invited by the visitor, she settles beside the sympathizer and accepts the strokes she thrives on. But when strangers leave, she leaps from the couch and prances off with even steps. Raja is a con artist.

All of us are a little like Raja. We have a certain idea of how God must prove His love for us. When He does not respond with the signs we expect, we often doubt our status and His love. *Am I really God's child? Does He really care about me?* Like Raja, we may even vie for attention by resorting to foolish tactics. The fact is, God's love for us never wavers, regardless of how things appear. And none of us needs to compete with another. God's love for humankind is equal toward all.

The Tail End

It will take an eternity to fully comprehend God's love.

The Bitter with the Sweet

*A*round one o'clock on an August morning, a couple from Illinois were driving Interstate 196, headed for their vacation in Grant, Michigan. Traveling in the minivan with them were two Westie terriers and two cats. As the driver approached road construction, the darkness made it easy to miss signs alerting him to the closed exit. The van slammed into a wall-high mound of crumbled concrete and clay, locking Eileen Walsh and her fiancé, Len Helbig, in the vehicle.

"Providentially," says Eileen, "our unreliable cell phone revived and Len was able to call paramedics. Maybe the jolt fixed it!" she jested. As serious as the collision was, Eileen maintained a sense of humor. "When Len reached out to protect my face, his hand encountered the potatoes au gratin that sailed out of our cooler, hit the windshield, and landed in my hair. A head of lettuce followed the potatoes, adding a green garnish to the concoction atop my head."

Eileen's lower body was shoved to the floor. Jammed side doors prevented easy access to her. Len waited with a broken ankle and lacerated nose until a rescue team arrived to break open the tailgate window. Four shocked animals also waited. The noisy Jaws of Life extraction tool sounded like jaws of terror for their cat, Murphy. When shattered glass finally opened a way of escape, he leaped through the window and fled.

Eileen and Len were hospitalized for several days, and the Southwestern Michigan Humane Society temporarily boarded their three rescued pets.

As soon as Eileen was released from the hospital, she placed an ad in area newspapers and printed "Lost Cat" fliers picturing Murphy, the black and white cat. She was amazed when a man who read the ad drove two hours to bring her a cat he found whose markings matched Murphy's. But the cat he pulled from his car was large and stout; Murphy was large and long. Eileen cried all night from the disappointment.

Another volunteer then joined the cast of players. Cyndy Winfield, owner of five cats, also saw the ad. Out of interest and compassion, she contacted Eileen. "We just clicked," said Winfield. Cyndy offered to help Eileen distribute fliers since she was acquainted with the area. She and two other volunteers went door to door with Eileen for over eight hours. Many contacts were negative. One woman brushed them off, speculating that area coyotes would surely have gobbled the cat by then. It had been three weeks since the accident. There were other naysayers, but Eileen kept hoping.

Meanwhile, retired schoolteachers Floyd and Barb Mattheeussen had noticed a cat on their property, just one-half mile from the exit where the accident had occurred. Floyd supposed it was a neighbor's. Later, Barb saw

the marauding cat not far from their bird feeder. She went outdoors and shooed him away.

Soon after, Eileen and her crew knocked on their door with a flier. Barb mentioned she had seen a similar cat but was unsure if he matched the picture. The cat's black half-mustache and skunk-like belly stripe distinguished him.

The following Sunday, a black and white cat showed up again at the Mattheeussen home. This time Barb tried the name. "C'mere Murphy," she coaxed. "He followed me right into our greenhouse and I quickly closed the door. He even let me pick him up. I put down a rug for him and drove to the store for cat food and litter," Barb said.

The Mattheeussens had not owned a cat for years due to Floyd's allergies, but Floyd still has a personal fondness for felines. "Murphy was so affectionate and a real pur-r-rcat," he said, smiling.

Monday morning Barb called Eileen at her Chicago office. Eileen sent Cyndy to the Mattheeussens to identify Murphy and asked her to take his favorite lamb treats to test his response. She figured if the markings were right, and he went for the lamb treats, he was Murphy.

Cyndy was elated when she examined the cat. Though she had seen only pictures, she was certain he was Murphy. Cyndy accepted the Mattheeussens' invitation for Murphy to stay in their greenhouse until Eileen could come pick him up.

That evening was a double festivity. When Eileen, her fiancé, Cyndy and her husband arrived to claim the cat, Floyd served everyone chocolate cake in observance of Barb's sixty-sixth birthday, while Murphy feasted on lamb treats in celebration of his survival and safe return home.

Though he had lost a little weight, the declawed house cat had fended well for himself, considering he was a city fellow and suffered from a chronic urinary tract problem.

Eileen was amazed by the friendliness and commitment of the Benton Township folks—those who responded to the ad, one who drove miles with a "possible" Murphy, three who volunteered to pass out fliers, and the retirees who captured her cat. "To think they would care about Murphy like that, touched my heart. I offered a one hundred dollar reward to Floyd and Barb but they firmly declined it. However, Floyd readily accepted my homemade almond cheese cake in lieu of the money."

Life is a mixture of losses and compensations. The auto crash caused a series of losses—a damaged vehicle, injured bodies, time away from jobs, a squelched vacation, and a lost pet. But compensations were in balance—new friends, physical recovery, renewed faith in people, a safely returned pet, and a fresh awareness of God's goodness. When we suffer trials, we can always be thankful for the blessings that offset our losses.

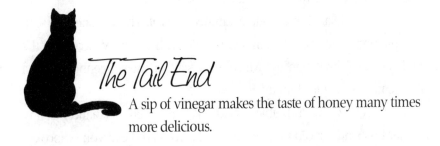

The Tail End

A sip of vinegar makes the taste of honey many times more delicious.

178

Contented as a Cat

Far away in the hills of Norway, Leif and his uncle Torkel worked hard on the family dairy farm. Out of kindness, they also assisted two spinsters who lived on an acreage adjacent to them. They often helped the sisters with harder manual chores, such as logging and splitting wood, and cutting the hay that grew on their steep hillside.

Inger and Emma preferred their solitary life. It may have felt like an intrusion when young Leif and his uncle arrived with a stockpile of wood or delivered a wagon load of hay. Visits with the ladies were few, though as a gesture of appreciation, the spinsters would invite them for meals. Emma was the cook, but sorely lacked culinary skills. Leif and Torkel were served a tasteless oatmeal gruel, bland meat and potato soup, and nondescript black bread. After a few experiences at their table, the hungry workers made excuses for declining dinner invitations.

The sisters were large-boned women with healthy, robust figures. Inger grew her hair long and slicked it back in a tightly knotted bun. Emma kept

179

hers clipped short and did little to groom it. The reclusive pair shared their life with two cats as inscrutable and introverted as they. Each cat had her domain; Svarten (meaning "the black one") lived outdoors, and Kjere ("the dear one") lived indoors.

When Torkel and Leif helped at the spinsters' farm, they would catch only quick glimpses of Svarten in the barnyard. She was as black as India ink, and as illusive as a shadow. Though rarely seen, she was always nearby. The quick cat darted from here to there, always crouched low and never close enough to grab. She would hide under a grain crate or leap to obscurity.

Svarten was a cat on assignment. Daily, she combed the property for mice and rats. Her belly bulged from a diet of abundant prey. Only when Emma set out a saucer of milk did Svarten emerge from her hideouts.

Svarten and Kjere served the women in ways that were as different as the colors of their fur—the service of one was practical and the service of the other was emotional. Svarten's job was hunting rodents and Kjere's job was dispensing affection.

On the occasions that Torkel and Leif dined with Emma and Inger, they observed Kjere. The pampered gray feline was skittish in the presence of strangers, but did not allow guests to keep her from the business of offering affection. As quickly as Emma settled on a chair, the loving cat jumped into her plump and sizable lap. Kjere would purr loudly, while turning her head in left and right motions of ecstasy. And though Leif and Torkel only ate small portions of Emma's victuals, Kjere complimented her cooking by gobbling every bite from the dish of table scraps.

Indoor Kjere and outdoor Svarten were each content in her sphere and in her service to the sisters. Though aware of one another, there was never a

hint that the cats were rivals. Torkel and Leif never saw Svarten meowing at the back door, pleading for entrance. And never did Kjere venture outside the door of the spinsters' large house.

Svarten was happy ambushing mice, spying on visitors, and breathing the air of changing seasons. The confinement of an indoor existence would have been stifling for the busy black cat. And Kjere was only mildly curious about the world existing beyond the four walls where she lazed and loved. From a window, she watched snowfall in winter and butterflies in summer but indicated no longing to do more than look. The cats were plainly content with the boundaries set for them.

Resigning to circumstances and yielding out of necessity is not equivalent to contentment. The contented heart accepts the perimeters that God appoints and revels in the realm of service God assigns.

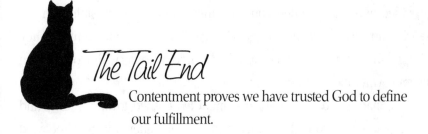

The Tail End

Contentment proves we have trusted God to define our fulfillment.

Cat, a Bird's Best Friend!

*S*haron never suspected a sundown stroll with her cat, Cleopatra, would one day involve a lifesaving interlude. The Siamese, nicknamed Cleo, is primarily an indoor cat, but enjoys a nightly walk with her owner through the field behind Sharon's home.

Cleo and Sharon often conclude their promenade by sitting on the hillside and watching the sunset. Their walks are seldom eventful. They simply share a time of quiet rest and outdoor scenery. But one spring evening was different from the rest.

As Sharon and Cleo ambled along, Cleo dashed toward a fence and peered down at something that captured her attention. She meowed repeatedly, excitedly. Sharon presumed Cleo had spotted an insect or a skittering mouse, so she made no effort to hurry toward her. When she reached Cleo, she had to look hard for the object that had aroused the cat's interest. She fumbled through some fallen leaves and then she saw it—a scrawny bundle of tiny wings and legs. She instantly recognized the species

of baby bird. Its russet shade and dark stripes were the color and markings of the California quail, one of Sharon's favorites.

"I stood there looking with Cleo, neither of us knowing what to do next. Cleo made no attempt to harm the bird or even draw closer. She was restless and appeared as concerned as I. She meowed occasionally, but kept turning to me as if to say, 'Well, do something!'"

Sharon sat down on the grass and began talking aloud, glancing at Cleo as if she understood every word. "*Now* what should I do? If I touch the bird, the parent may reject it. But maybe it's abandoned. It's almost dark and getting chilly. The animals that roam here at night will probably find the bird if I don't move it."

After wrestling through her thoughts, she said, "C'mon Cleo, let's call a wildlife rescue group and ask for advice."

Sharon telephoned a volunteer who explained that California quail are ground-nesting birds. She was told the chick was likely deserted only because the parents had been driven away. "Unattended, the bird probably won't survive the night," warned the volunteer. "Can you bring it to me?"

"Oh yes, if you think you can help!" Sharon was hopeful and relieved.

She found a small box and lined it with crumpled paper. Armed with a flashlight she headed back to the field and lifted the hapless bird into the container. Her husband offered to drive them to the volunteer's home.

Upon examination, the bird was judged healthy. "It seems to be in pretty good shape. I'm caring for thirty other birds, but I'll gladly take one more," said the volunteer, as she rushed away to select appropriate food for the trembling quail. Sharon and her husband left the bird and drove home with a feeling of commendation.

Sharon later pondered the rare string of events—a cat had led to the rescue and salvation of a bird—an extraordinary occurrence between predator and prey. Thanks to Cleo's keen smell and sharp eyesight, at least one bird in Santa Clara County has a feline for a best friend.

If the quail had hoped to chance upon someone for assistance that night, it would not have wished for a cat. Yet those we presume are against us, sometimes become our biggest advocates. A high school enemy may turn out to be a best friend in adulthood. A college professor we most feared may become our son or daughter's role model. Such turnabouts in life are among the pleasant surprises God brings into our lives. Don't be smug in your predictions about encounters. You might be as surprised as a California quail!

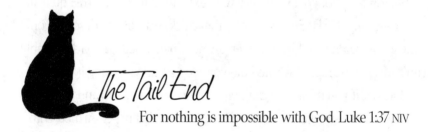

The Tail End

For nothing is impossible with God. Luke 1:37 NIV

Campus Cats

$\mathcal{C}$ats have a way of achieving access to high places, particularly those on rooftops and tall trees. The cats belonging to the Eastern Washington University president and his wife are among felines who illustrate the rags to riches scenario. Even cosmetic disadvantages failed to hinder the cats in their rise to the top.

This tale of two cats began when Dr. Stephen Jordan and his wife Ruth moved to Topeka, Kansas. After settling in their new home, they decided to adopt two cats. Their elderly kitty had passed away and the children were now grown and gone.

Word spread of Ruth's plans to find two kittens. She and Stephen had casually looked but discovered the month of January was not a time when kittens are plentiful.

One day the doorbell rang. Ruth opened the door to find a woman holding a cardboard box filled with five kittens. The happy presenter was Dr.

Jordan's secretary. "Ruth, I found just what you've been searching for!" Certain her delivery was the fulfillment of Ruth's wishes, she was ecstatic.

However, the specific selection of a pet is a personal matter. Like choosing the color of a new car or the pattern on wallpaper, most owners are particular about their choice of a cat's markings. Ruth was nonplused when she looked at the mewing litter. Not one kitten fit any standard category of description. Tabby?–well, partly. Calico?–only the head. Coal black?–Except for the tail that was streaked with burnt orange. None were classic or beautiful.

"Oh, please come in," Ruth graciously answered. Curious about the uncomely genre of felines, she asked, "Where did you find them?"

"They're the latest litter from our barn cat," explained the lady, quite cheerfully.

Ruth felt cornered. The goodwill of the secretary was plain. But Ruth was not the least bit attracted to any of the oddly colored kittens, and there was no way out.

"Let me take a closer look," said Ruth, as she reached for one kitten and then another, holding it up, turning it in her hands, and trying to decide on the best two. Without voicing her frustration, she finally realized there were no "best two." None was more lovely or less irregular than another. So she picked out a pair and the transaction was done.

"Thank you for thinking of us," Ruth said.

"I knew you'd be thrilled," said the caller. *Thrilled* was hardly an accurate description of Ruth's reaction. But behind the tightly closed door of Ruth's mind, she told herself that a cat was a cat, and the feelings of the sincere secretary were more important than the color of a cat.

When Stephen came home that evening, Ruth introduced him to the new family members. His response matched hers when she had glanced into the box earlier that day. "Don't say anything, Stephen. I know what you're thinking. But we'll grow to love them. I'm warming up to them already. You will, too."

Dr. Jordan, Director for the Board of Regents over six state universities in Kansas, had weightier concerns, indeed. But he shook his head, though smiling, as he viewed the strangely colored kitten who ran to his feet.

Ruth named the barnyard cats Thelma and Louise. Thelma, shy and fearful, soon gravitated toward Stephen, quickly winning his affections; and Louise, social and friendly, favored Ruth. In little time, the delightful presence of the spirited kittens abolished all awareness of their physical charm—or the lack of it.

Advancement from a barn to the fine residence of a professional was only the beginning for Thelma and Louise. In 1998, Dr. Jordan accepted the presidential position at EWU in Cheney, Washington. The Washington state legislature required its new leader to live in the Cheney community, so the Jordans began to make plans for their move.

Dr. Jordan's three predecessors had chosen to live off campus. Thus, the original two-story brick home built for the college president was in need of refurbishing. Over $125,000 was spent remodeling the 1929 home that combined Colonial and Georgian architectures, with its signature row of white columns around the porch. Thelma and Louise now sunbathe on window ledges that are molded and cased in dark tiger oak. Unlike most barn cats, they claim a territory of blond tongue-and-groove oak floors decorated with oriental carpets. They pass through wood doors with inlaid pinstripes and chase one another up a staircase that makes two ninety-degree turns as it ascends to the bedrooms.

Ruth also hired an interior decorator. "We wanted a home . . . ," she said, " . . . a warm place to entertain." Since completion of the renovation, the Jordans have hosted hundreds of guests. Receptions and dinner parties have included the occasional appearance of Thelma and Louise. Ruth says, "The cats have adapted very well. Throughout the transition, we've given them extra love."

The Jordans have particularly enjoyed restoring the house and becoming an integral part of campus life. Thelma and Louise have also integrated with the university district. After all, every school needs campus cats. Ruth says it is hard to believe she was even slightly reluctant to accept the two felines who have become such a welcome part of their lives. "We're truly attached."

Thelma and Louise's journey from a cardboard box to their historic home is not a feline fable. The uncomely kittens amounted to more than what met the eye. Inward character will always outweigh external adornment. And what is on the inside of both cats and people is the stuff that takes us to higher planes.

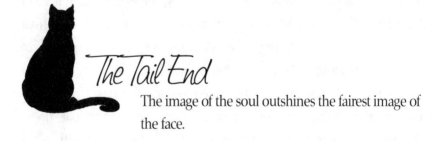

The image of the soul outshines the fairest image of the face.

Closed Doors

One balmy spring evening Jane settled on the sofa beside her husband, Jack, to watch the late news. Before she had a chance to rest her feet on the footstool, she heard one of the cats meow her request to come indoors. She rose and opened the door. To Jane's chagrin, she then heard their dog scratch *his* wishes to come inside. Annoyed, she went to the door a second time. Twice more she played gatekeeper for the family pets while trying to view footage of world events.

It was early in the season, before flies and bugs swarm the house if the door is left ajar. Jane decided to leave open the glass slider so her animal population could come and go without her assistance. Thirty minutes later, she turned off the television and closed the slider. She and Jack headed for bed.

On the verge of sleep, Jane felt a cat jump on her feet. Then the cat lunged again, only a few inches from her toes. She bolted upright to see her jumping from one spot to another. *Funny,* she thought, *Behzheka hasn't done*

189

that since she was a kitten. Again the cat jolted the bed with a pounce. Now fully awakened and clear-minded, Jane realized Behzheka was aware of something under the covers other than her still-sleeping husband.

The scenario continued. Jane shrieked when she and Behzheka saw the next "under-cover" movement. Jack turned wide-eyed and looked baffled as Jane leaped from bed and flipped on the light switch. He remained speechless as she threw back the blankets. Uncovered, they beheld a confused gray mouse scurrying across the bed. Behzheka sprang upon the mouse in determined pursuit! Even Jane's screaming failed to distract the excited cat.

At last Jack joined the action. He captured the mouse with gloved hand and disposed of it outside. He grabbed Behzheka and told her the outdoors would be a more suitable jungle-style setting for her mouseketeer expeditions. As he padded barefooted back to the bedroom, Jane changed the sheets. It was almost an hour before Jane stopped "feeling" things move under the covers and relaxed enough to drift off to sleep.

Behzheka will always be a hunter. The small black, gray and white striped cat had been found starving in an alley in Moscow, Russia. Her rescuer, a student who later shared an apartment with Jane's daughter, brought Behzheka to the United States. Behzheka was spayed and had her forepaws declawed after her arrival. Unhindered, she still catches mice using her sharp back claws.

Since the cat and mouse episode, Behzheka gets a thorough frisking when she steps through the door. Jane and Jack were not amused by "what the cat drug in," but they learned something valuable. The Open Door Policy is no longer in effect at their house.

Their experience is a good reminder that doors swing two ways. They open to allow entrance and they close to secure privacy. Doors signify a boundary line by regulating what comes in and what goes out. Jane and Jack lifted a boundary and ended up with an undesirable bed companion. If we live life failing to establish physical, emotional, and social boundaries we invite disturbances, both small and large.

The Tail End

An open door doesn't always mean you're invited in.

The Preeminence of Love

*P*arented from prestigious stock, Oliver was the offspring of a new mix. But the Burmese kitten was a disappointment to his breeder only moments after his birth. Speckled across his shoulders were a few white hairs which disqualified him as a potential show cat. Little did the breeder know what potential lay within his "imperfect" kitten.

Dean and Cathy Anderson were at the top of the breeder's list of prospective buyers. Fortunately, they were waiting to adopt a Burmese kitten, not a show cat. The selection of a Burmese had not been without Cathy's studious comparison with other exotics. The stocky round-chested Burmese are exceptionally affectionate, the virtue that influenced Cathy's choice.

Though their new kitten would never parade before judges, he was born for a mission far more important. He would, however, receive a name that suited his fine bloodline. Because he made grand leaps accentuated by a little twist, the Andersons named him Oliver Twist. For the sake of brevity, he became Oliver.

From the beginning, Oliver loved everyone. He spread his affection evenly among family members, leaving evidence of his loving presence with sable brown hairs (and occasionally, a disqualifying white one!) shed at the foot of each of their beds.

Just 12 months before Oliver arrived, Dean had been diagnosed with life-threatening cancer. Tests confirmed the shocking news only three days before Dean's own father died of cancer. Oliver would journey with Dean through the next six and a half years as he battled for life.

Dean began traditional treatment. But three years later, the disease had progressed, forcing him to leave his medical practice. Oliver sensed Dean's acute change in health and migrated toward him with keen sensitivity.

When radiation, chemotherapy, and experimental treatments diminished Dean's strength, two naps a day became routine. Oliver tripped upstairs to the bedroom with Dean for each session of respite. Dean would call, "Come, cat!" As the months passed, it was Oliver who summoned Dean to the stairway. He was as constant a support as the pillow under Dean's head. With golden eyes tightly closed, Oliver would slumber under Dean's upper arm.

"Oliver's companionship comforted not only Dean," said Cathy, "but I too was comforted knowing Dean was not entirely alone when I was called from his side." When years of failed drugs and procedures left Dean's body consumed by the advancing cancer cells, his attentive family and faithful kitty began living with the imminence of his passing.

Soon after his diagnosis, Dean had begun a quest to know God. He who had sailed his own boats, flown his own planes, skied, golfed, traveled, and enjoyed both professional success and a circle of extraordinary friends, sensed something fundamental was missing in his life. But his newfound relationship with God enhanced his final years and prepared him for a premature death.

In Dean's final week, his mind was troubled from large doses of pain-suppressing drugs and his fifty-eight-year-old body fought for continuing life. He mumbled in his sleep, and tossed in his bed. Oliver stayed away. The solid nine-pound cat was agitated and tense, prancing through the house, seemingly undone. But in Dean's last hours, his body relaxed, and Oliver joined him once more. When Dean passed away, Oliver was asleep, curled at his feet. Cathy, her children, and the nurse all noticed. Oliver's exemplary calm was symbolic of the peace Dean now enjoyed.

The following morning, Cathy faced the worst pain of losing her husband of twenty-two years. "I was overwhelmed with grief. I stumbled outside to the bedroom deck and unwittingly left the door ajar. Oliver followed behind. Finding no relief, I returned to the bedroom and rocked myself on the edge of the bed. I gripped my arms, helpless with hurt. Oliver, who had found a tiny pine cone on the deck, brought it inside and dropped it at my feet. He wanted to play fetch. In a perfunctory response, I threw it for him, and he brought it back. I threw it again, and heard myself chuckle. At that moment, I knew Oliver's loving ministrations would continue as we began a new life without husband and father."

And so it has been. Dean and Cathy's son, James, drops in from the nearby college to do his laundry, to check on his mom, and to get his love fix from Oliver. Marisa, their daughter, hunts for Oliver as soon as she steps through the door after school. The still youthful Oliver has become more

active, but when he sleeps, he chooses the chair that now has replaced the hospital bed.

In reflections written by Dean and read at his memorial service, he referred to the words of Jesus. To Martha, Jesus said, "Only one thing is needful," meaning, the love of God. To the rich young ruler, Jesus said, "One thing you lack," again inferring, the love of God. Through his suffering Dean had come to understand what was centrally important in life—things truly needful and too often lacking—love for God and for people.

One thing is essential for each of us. For Oliver, it was not "show cat acclaim." Instead, Oliver faithfully served a dying man with the devotion of love, a gift not lacking in the heart of the little brown cat. May none of us be deficient in love for God and humankind—it is primary in life and enduring in death.

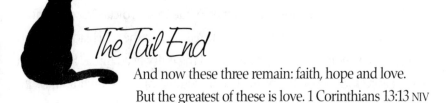

The Tail End

And now these three remain: faith, hope and love.
But the greatest of these is love. 1 Corinthians 13:13 NIV

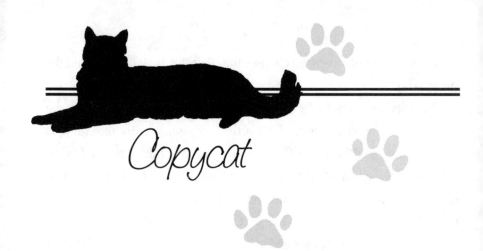

Copycat

Susan's seven-year-old sister chirped her announcement as she held forth a shiny black kitten. "Mommy, I found a new friend!"

At once Susan's mother, Jessie, began her "no cats" rhetoric. "You shouldn't have brought the kitty home, Cindy. You need to return it right now. You know Dad won't approve."

The baby face of the irresistible kitten made Jessie's dictates sound harsh. As quickly as she finished her lecture, she reached for the coal black puff, and dropped into her rocking chair. She tucked the fluffy head under her chin. In one forward rock, Jessie knew she had joined the camp that would rally for the kitten when her husband came home.

Susan stood by whining. "Let *me* hold her!" Cindy warmed a bowl of milk.

"I named her Midnight," said Cindy.

"Well, remember, we have to see what your father says." Jessie placed Midnight beside the bowl of milk. As Susan settled on the floor and stroked Midnight's silky spine, she knew the kitten would stay.

Midnight was about four months old with a black velvet nose and eyes like emeralds. In the center of her chest, she wore a dozen white hairs that bedecked her like a tiny locket. Midnight would receive double-takes all her life.

"'You know you're gorgeous, Midnight,' was Mom's repeated compliment in the years that followed," said Susan. "She would sit in the picture window framed by ruffled curtains and often stretched her graceful length on our blue floral rug. 'Look at me,' she seemed to say. She would fix herself on the top of our best wingback chair, posed like an onyx sphinx waiting for homage. Mom used to say Midnight's life mission was to display her uncommon elegance for the recognition and applause of admirers."

Six months after her arrival, Midnight presented the family with her first and only litter. None of the assorted mix of black, white, and gray kittens elicited her motherly attention.

"What a rotten mother!" Jessie had exclaimed. Midnight batted her squeaking kittens when they tried in vain to nurse. While they hung tightly to her teats, she stood and walked away until each kitten finally let go and dropped to the floor. While the kittens cried for her milk, she munched her food with indifference. As soon as the kittens were able to leave the basket, Midnight officially abandoned them. She paid no attention to them unless to hiss at one for nibbling from her food dish. The family prevented the abuse of later litters by spaying her, an act for which Midnight was likely grateful.

They wondered if Midnight had been deprived of a normal mother model to copy—a plausible theory since they later learned she was a first class copycat.

Several years later, the family moved. Midnight was no longer free to roam the neighborhood. Cloistered in a tiny upstairs apartment, she got her first introduction to a litter box.

One morning, Jessie climbed back in bed after her husband and children left for the day. Before long, she heard a tinkling sound coming from the bathroom.

"Charlie, is that you? I thought you'd gone," she called. But there was no answer. She presumed the toilet was running. Midnight hopped to the foot of the bed and they both drifted off to sleep.

A week later, Jessie heard the familiar sound once again. With her hands full of breakfast dishes, she stopped to listen. She put the dishes in the sink and headed for the bathroom. *Why didn't I tell Charlie to fix that toilet,* she thought. Her intention was to jiggle the handle.

Jessie reached the bathroom doorway and was met by Midnight's neon eyes. There sat the cat, squatted purposefully on the toilet seat. Astounded, Jessie watched her tinkle and afterwards claw at the toilet paper in an attempt to pull a strip across the seat. Then she stepped off and waltzed past Jessie, offering a passing rub with her usual cool affection.

Susan remembers her mother's surprise that day. "Mom was waiting at the door when we burst in after school. 'You'll never believe what Midnight is doing!'" she said. "All of us were anxious to hear."

She related her incredulous story and got an incredulous response. "Yeah, sure, Mom, you're not only hearing tinkling sounds, now you're seeing things!" The kids teased her as they snacked on macaroons. Curious, however, they waited and watched.

198

During the next few days, each family member caught Midnight practicing her new skill. The tissue did not always make it across the seat, but the family commended her for the fastidious effort.

"It was amazing enough that she mimicked our toilet habits, but her use of the toilet tissue, though in a manner different from ours, was her crowning achievement. We half expected her to start flushing!" said Susan.

Like Midnight, every person is somewhat of a copycat. We imitate what we observe in others—sometimes the bad, sometimes the good. Midnight was likely a poor mother because she had a poor role model. But she picked up her good toilet habits by watching positive models. There is no copyright on exemplary behavior. Copying good examples perpetuates high standards, worthy traditions, and lofty values.

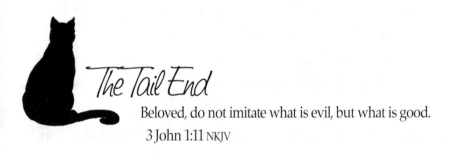

The Tail End

Beloved, do not imitate what is evil, but what is good.
3 John 1:11 NKJV

The Taming of Mother

$\mathcal{O}$ne summer morning as Leah approached the door of the Chalet Family Restaurant, she noticed a tiny kitten peeking out from under the foundation of the adjacent store. Leah walked to the small opening, and stooped to look. Crouched in fear were two cats and three kittens.

Leah hastened inside and ordered a hamburger—for the cats. The cook knew her and quickly fried a patty. Leah returned to the cats' hiding place and held out the meat. They snatched the burger and scratched her hand. Thus began an unusual eleven-year relationship with the female cat who spent most of her life under the store.

The next morning, Leah drove to the Chalet with chopped liver and canned and dry cat food. She slid the food under the foundation, went into the restaurant for coffee, and afterwards collected the empty cat dishes. This routine continued the next few days. By the fourth day, the cats stopped raking her hand. In the following weeks, Leah would arrive with

their food and honk. The cats poked their heads from the hole and waited for the handout.

During winter, Leah brought them a low box padded with a blanket and shoved it underneath the dark and spidered home of her "bag cats." She also added an extra evening visit to give them water that was not frozen.

A humorous thing happened while she cared for the feral cats. One day she spotted the adult female, whom she named Mother, on the rooftop of the restaurant. She was meowing, as if stranded. While restaurant customers crowded around her, Leah stood on the walkway looking up and calling, "Mother! Mother, do you need help?" A puzzled gentleman tapped her on the shoulder and asked, "Ma'am, is your mother up there?"

By now, Leah was used to curious questioners. Many had watched her on hands and knees supplying food and retrieving dishes at the foundation edge, and calling the fortunate strays by name. "No sir, it's a cat," she said, with no further explanation. He left bemused.

In January, she began thinking about catching the cats to have them spayed and neutered. She had determined which one was the mother and that the larger one was a tomcat. The kittens needed to be altered too. In February, she took a springform trap to the cat site and baited it with liver. It took three weeks to catch all five cats. The alley-wise mother was the last to be captured. Leah took them directly to the vet. The five cats were so wild, the veterinarian had to tranquilize them.

A client in the clinic overheard Leah's story and asked to adopt the tomcat. Leah was elated. She returned the four other cats to their familiar home, and continued to feed them twice a day. She planned to catch them again before winter, when they would be more tame.

That fall, she caught the three kittens and took them home for good. But even withholding a feeding was not enough to tempt the mother. No method Leah tried outwitted her. One failed attempt after another required Leah to continue her daily food deliveries. Amidst her rescue efforts, the demands of life continued. At times it seemed easier to bring food than to contend with Mother's opposition. So, for the next eleven years, Leah brought her food—in subzero temperatures, and even when the town was deep in ash from a volcanic eruption.

As if the resistance from Mother was not enough to overcome, Leah was also scorned one day by a long-haired, bearded man who saw her reaching under the foundation. He asked what she was doing. Leah explained politely, after which he muttered, "You should be feeding starving people in Bangladesh, not cats!"

Leah said she donated to several charities and cared enough about people to volunteer at the hospital for twenty-three years. "Maybe you should go home and read the Bible; it says we are also to care for animals," she advised. When the man called her a religious fanatic, she refrained from further conversation and he left.

Many years later, the vet's assistant volunteered to help Leah try once again to catch Mother. An ambush was set up. The assistant arrived early and waited at the opening, out of sight. Leah drove up and honked, and the helper grabbed Mother when she ran forward for food. Mother was nabbed, but in her struggle to go free, the frantic cat shredded the assistant's sweater.

Leah took Mother home and put her in the basement where she could be alone in a warm screened room with food, water, and litter. Through the screen, she could see Leah's other cats, some of whom were her offspring.

The frightened cat did not eat, drink, or use the litter box from Thursday until Monday. It was a year and a half before she was brave enough to join Leah and the other cats upstairs, though they spent time with her each day. Thanks to Leah, the final six years of Mother's life were a dramatic contrast to her earlier existence.

Leah was not dissuaded by the taunts of people who would rather criticize another person's efforts than find and pursue a goal of their own. Bystanders judged Leah's nurture of the cats in a variety of ways. She was tagged weird, fanatic, and lonely, although some admired her. When we believe our goals are worthwhile, the opinions of others should not discourage us. Their ridicule is meddlesome. It is we who endure the consequences but also reap the advantages of our projects. Hush the critics! Hurrah for the Leahs!

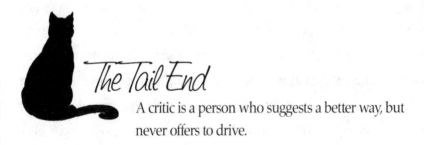

The Tail End

A critic is a person who suggests a better way, but never offers to drive.

Upbringing

Sophie sighed. "Tsk! The rural life!" Mick, her owner, sensed Sophie's disgust. The all-white cat was not enchanted with the wheat farm where her family had recently moved. She finished her inspection of the farmhouse, then pushed open the unlatched screen. She took two cautious steps and stood for a panoramic view of the countryside.

Where were the sidewalks? Had the county run short of funds, she wondered? She was aghast at the tall, untamed grass, a sure sign of neglect. And to her right, she caught sight of three imposing animals that struggled in their attempt to greet her with a meow. The closest they came to a proper feline hello was "Moo." Sophie glanced upward at Mick. She obviously hoped the monstrous animals, with their poor communication skills, were not permanent residents.

"Go on, Sophie, take a look out there. This place is a city dweller's dream!" Mick knew he sounded pushy. Reluctantly, Sophie headed out to

explore this "dream" place. Mick was not surprised when his city cat returned shortly thereafter.

Eventually, Sophie would get a real taste of the country and still be unimpressed. Within the next few days, she grew bolder and stalked the cows, studied the horses, and investigated a multitude of new and strange noises. After the rural phenomena became halfway tolerable, Mick spotted Sophie conducting an outdoor foray. Mick was seated in the breakfast nook and through the window he was privy to Sophie's adventure.

Her attention was suddenly seized by a trembling shrub. Simultaneously, Mick and Sophie both saw a little red robin in the bush, jumping from one twig to another. All of Sophie's ancestral instincts overcame her gentle city breeding. She who had never known the pangs of hunger nor stalked anything more than a pet shop cat toy, instantly turned into a huntress. She lowered her haunches, vibrated her tail and positioned herself for attack.

She leaped! And then, like a kamikaze pilot, she headed downward for a doomed landing. All the grace associated with felines was amusingly absent in her descent. She hit the ground tumbling in an unplanned somersault. Only one thing saved her pride. She collided with the bird and captured it between her teeth. Mick noticed her eyes were filled with bewilderment.

What do I do now? was her unspoken thought as she looked left and then right, hoping someone nearby would give her advice. For lack of any guidance, she tore off around a corner of the house.

"I would certainly have gained no points had Sophie heard me laughing, but I could hardly contain myself," said Mick. "I really wanted to know what would happen next. So, with great self-control, I tiptoed to the door and

looked, just as she was coming around the opposite corner. In the time it had taken her to cover the distance of only one house length, she had fully gained control of the situation."

Unfortunately, not even a successful catch improved Sophie's view of the glorified image of rural existence. Sophie did not like birds or the country. Her ten years of high society breeding had shaped her preferences for life. She spit out the bird at Mick's feet, along with a couple of loose feathers, then darted between his legs and ran to her kitchen bowl for a meal-size portion of Kitty Krunchies. The unharmed bird rolled to his feet and flew to safety. Sophie never again hunted bush wigglers and never adjusted to the countrified meow of the cows. Like child rearing, cat rearing lasts for a lifetime.

Even animals can be affected positively by their upbringing. The influence of environment, the molding of education, the training of loving parents, and the guidelines of faith enable us to live above base instincts that might otherwise drive us to shameful actions. Never believe the lie that "you just can't help yourself." Humankind can resist the instincts of hate, rage, and destruction in the same way a city cat spits out a bird.

The Tail End

Parents need never doubt the lasting influence of a proper upbringing.

Long-Suffering's Reward

When Jane Harris watched her daughter reach for the homeliest kitten in the litter of eligible Siamese, she winced. Though the uncomely cat boasted prestigious papers, she was the last one Jane would have picked from the mewing huddle of kittens. Jane tried to persuade her daughter, Megan, and her sons, Mark and Jason, to consider choosing a different cat from among the pool of hopefuls, but Megan became instantly attached to the unsightly female she named Katie.

Home they went with a cat. Although Katie was far from adorable in appearance, the family also soon discovered that she was not even personable. Unlike the loving cat Megan had hoped for, Katie barely tolerated everyone in the family, with the exception of Mark. In the years to come, Megan would shed many disappointed tears over Katie's rejection of her.

Because the Harrises had paid a substantial price and made a commitment, they kept the temperamental cat. Katie's partiality for Mark was their only consolation. The rest of the family merely cohabited with

Katie, who continually rebuffed their affectionate gestures. The cranky little cat shunned laps, wiggled out of arms longing to cradle her, and seldom purred. Her attitude toward people was one of disdainful tolerance.

As for her response to strangers, Katie was simply rude. If a smiling visitor reached out to pet her, she would swipe the kindly intentioned hand and sometimes even scratch. During Katie's first thirteen years with the family, Jane made more excuses for Katie's behavior than she ever did for her children's. Nonetheless, as the months became years, the family learned to love Katie in spite of her indifference to them and her blatant unwillingness to give much in return to anyone but Mark.

The day arrived when Mark reached young adulthood and left for college. Katie grieved for awhile, but soon refocused her devotion on Jason with surprising fidelity. To Jason's amazement, Katie took to his lap, allowed him to hold her, and now slept at the foot of his bed. Jason was pleased, but Megan viewed it as yet another rejection. Some years earlier, however, Jane had allowed Megan to have another cat whom Katie tolerated in much the same style she did the rest of the family—peaceful, but disinterested, coexistence.

Katie aged along with the maturing children. When she was thirteen she began to show signs of failure. A trip to the vet did not reveal any serious problems, although Katie was losing weight and appeared frail. A weeping eye was treated with an ointment, but began discharging again soon after antibiotics were stopped.

One Saturday when Jane was home alone, she paid particular attention to Katie who began the day sleeping on the back of the couch. The suffering little cat did not move for twelve hours. Something was seriously wrong. Jane chauffeured Katie to the vet and requested a thorough exam. To everyone's

dismay, a tumor originating behind Katie's eye was growing through her cornea—a very painful condition. Since she was an elderly kitty, the vet asked if they would prefer to put Katie to sleep. The family discussed the predicament and everyone agreed that the risks of surgery were worth a chance of saving Katie. The removal of her eye was successfully completed by sewing the lid closed. Katie was finally ready to go home, minus one eye and no longer in pain, but the family could never have anticipated the unseen changes being worked in their ill-tempered cat.

If ever adversity affected a change of heart, Katie's crisis changed her into a new creature! The family marveled. Who was this loving feline? Had the vet counseled her? Had she experienced a new birth? Or was she just glad to be free of pain? Only Katie knows how long the tumor had tormented her or affected her personality. Before Katie was fully recovered, it was obvious that although she had lost 50 percent of her eyesight, she had gained some extraordinary insight. She was now affectionate with everyone—even strangers were greeted with her seven pound person lighting upon their laps. Katie suddenly expressed her undying appreciation for the faithful family that had chosen her, ugly though she was, had endured her aloof and unresponsive behavior for years, and most recently had relieved her pain and spared her life with a costly operation.

Many adjustments were soon made in the Harris home—for both cat and family. Katie had to learn to perceive her world with one eye. She had trouble aiming her mouth into the food dish and often spilled her tidbits or bumped her chin on the dish rim. She would leap to a desktop and land where she hadn't intended. In time, though, she adapted to navigating with one eye and began functioning normally.

The adjustment for the family was a more pleasant kind; they were living with the new blessing of a delightful cat. She purred nonstop and consented to hugs, strokes, and kisses. Jane marvels, "Our once distant cat became so affectionate, now she's sometimes a nuisance."

At fourteen, Katie is free of ailments and full of love. Fourteen years was a long time to wait for signs of gratefulness from someone in whom the Harrises had made a lifetime investment of love. But they never regretted choosing Katie, their feisty feline turned happy devotee. Recompense may have been awhile in coming, but they learned that long-awaited rewards can be that much sweeter!

The Tail End

Victories quickly won are not nearly so rewarding as victories won through patience, endurance, and trial.

A Simple Saint

When a black and white female kitten arrived on the ten-acre country parcel owned by a registered nurse, the cat could hardly have anticipated the destiny that lay ahead for her. Little did she know that she would become the resident pet at an extended care facility, ministering special comfort to an extended family of patients.

Kaye Conrath, R.N. at St. Luke's Extended Care, fed the skinny stray a can of tuna but kept her outside. The homeless cat was still hanging around when Kaye and her husband went on vacation. Kaye then made a statement, not a request, to her spouse. "If the cat is still here when we get back, we'll adopt her." The insistent kitten was patiently waiting on the porch when they returned. A friend persuaded Kaye to first have the cat examined by a vet. Ear mites were treated, vaccines injected, and front paws were declawed. The amount of the bill settled any outstanding questions of ownership. She now irrevocably belonged to Kaye.

Soon after, St. Luke's began discussing the possibility of adopting a cat. "I've got a perfect kitty in mind," said Kaye. "She's affectionate, small, and declawed." The administration welcomed Kaye's applicant and hired her after one purr.

St. Luke's has a progressive view on the benefits of pet therapy. Audra, a recreational therapist aide, said, "This is home for our patients. A resident cat makes it even more so." The care center also has fish and a cockatoo, and allows family members or friends to bring pets to visit.

Soon after the cat arrived, the staff held a "Name-the-Cat" contest. The repeated suggestion was "Luke," a fitting name at St. Luke's Extended Care Center, but not very suitable for a female. Everyone agreed the name "Lucy" was close enough. Like all newly arrived residents, a poster of Lucy was soon featured on the bulletin board with her picture, interests, and life history. Lucy quickly won the hearts of the residents—even those who before gave their allegiance only to dogs. "Where's Lucy?" or, "How's Lucy today?" became their frequent inquiries.

Several hurdles related to health regulations needed to be overcome before Lucy could be admitted. The fact that residents might have dander allergies needed to be addressed. That issue was easily dismissed by the fact that floors are mopped twice a day removing fur and dander from areas where Lucy traffics. The matter of a sanitary setup for Lucy's litter box was handled next. The husband of a social worker built the custom chest that houses a large tub of litter. A swinging door allows Lucy access and the hinged lid makes it easy to remove the tub to refill or wash. (Audra decorated the white painted container with pastel flowers.) A third concern were Lucy's claws. To protect the fragile skin of patients, Lucy's rear feet were also

declawed. With no enemies inside the walls of St. Luke's, her ministrations to patients are only enhanced by her soft paws. Lucy's safety was the final challenge. She was outfitted with an inch-square proximity alarm attached to her collar. If she goes too near a door leading outside, the alarm sounds, alerting the staff.

Lucy's days are now filled with activity. When the recreational therapist sets up the hallway for bowling, Lucy joins the game. She maneuvers around the pins and avoids the rolling ball. At other times, she leaps to the top of the covered linen cart as the laundress shuttles it from room to room. The ride offers Lucy a bit of excitement and an elevated perspective. But her favorite amusement is watching wild birds feed from feeders that hang outdoors. From one of the larger offices with tall windows, she sits nose-to-glass and fantasizes about life beyond the transparent barrier!

Testimonies from residents prove that Lucy has brought her own special brand of healing to the ill and recovering. One patient's daughter recently died. The grieving father slipped into a depression and wore a sour expression—until Lucy visited him. It was the first time he had smiled since he received the heartbreaking news of his daughter's passing.

Keith, a gentleman whose room is at the end of the hallway, receives an occasional visit from Lucy who hops into a chair and naps while Keith plays video games. "I like company, even if it's a cat. When Lucy comes, I don't feel so isolated."

Pam has lost the use of her arms. Since she misses the gratification of stroking cats, she is delighted when staff members pick Lucy up and set her close by.

The second floor at St. Luke's is for transitional patients—those who will go home after rehabilitation. Shelley, a beautiful and bright-eyed young woman who was born with cerebral palsy, underwent surgery to have her tendons and heel cords lengthened. The procedure would free her from the knock-knee condition that had caused her to fall and shatter her tailbone. She was placed in a full body cast that left her feeling claustrophobic. In the early days of recovery, she struggled with the physical restraint and the emotional impact. "I'm otherwise healthy, so the confinement of the cast was awful. I was ready to give up. Then a nurse brought me Lucy. She walked around my body and tiptoed to my chin. Petting Lucy somehow made a difference. She's a special little cat," said Shelley.

St. Luke, the ancient physician, would be pleased with the loving and quality care offered at the extended care center named after him. Many would say that now there is a modern-day saint wandering the halls—an unlikely saint of the most humble size and sort—Lucy, the cat. She has no training, holds no certification, and loses no sleep over the stresses and difficulties of life. She serves effectively by simply being herself. Pur-r-rhaps there's a lesson in that for us all.

The Tail End

There is no salve for the sick so healing as the unaffected simplicity of our caring presence.

Forgiveness Brings Warmth

*T*he mercies of a pet rescue organization halted the doom of euthanasia for three orange tabbies my husband and I would later adopt. We first spotted the three males in a display cage at a pet store the afternoon we were shopping for a sibling pair. A coyote had recently killed our beloved ten-year-old Thurlough as he roamed the golf course behind our home. Rather than expose our new pets to the danger of predators and a nearby busy thoroughfare, we decided our future felines would be confined indoors. Thus, we wanted two cats so each would have a companion.

We signed adoption papers within an hour of our introduction to Earl and Murray, the two we agreed to purchase. But we would have to wait a couple of days to take them home. The sales agreement required that the cats be neutered before their release to the adoptive family. Their rescuer and foster parent took Earl, Murray, and also Myles, to the veterinarian for their scheduled alteration. The following afternoon I arrived at the clinic, claimed my two kittens, and brought them home. But the next day . . .

Myles was fightin' mad! He arrived at our home twenty-four hours after his two siblings, Earl and Murray. All three kittens had been neutered and were waiting at the veterinary clinic, but we had arranged to bring home only two. Myles was returned to his foster home, while Earl and Murray came home with us. The separation was tough for Myles, and recovering from surgery without Earl and Murray was even worse.

I was the dissenter who thought three kittens was one too many, but the following day I reconsidered. My husband's appeal to "keep the brothers together" finally weakened my resolve. Ecstatic, he hurried to the phone to arrange for the adoption of Myles.

Presuming the kitten reunion would be a happy event, we were anxious to reunite the three brothers. Contrary to our expectations, Myles spit, hissed, swatted, and refused the welcome from Earl and Murray. We were bewildered, until we remembered he was recovering from the discomfort of surgery and his temporary rejection. The introduction to strange surroundings did not help his mood.

That first evening was tense for everyone. Myles declined invitations from his brothers for playful wrestling and huddled by himself in an obvious furor of unforgiveness. "Poor little fellow," commented my husband, "I guess he wants someone to blame."

The next morning we were relieved to find Myles sleeping in a furry pile between his siblings. Apparently he decided that blaming was not much fun and being together again was what he wanted all along. Forgiving his brothers for their temporary desertion made his night warmer and the new day brighter.

There are no platitudes asserting that forgiveness is easy. It is perhaps the hardest moral act humans accomplish. Only the magnitude of God's forgiveness toward us can inspire and enable us to forgive those who hurt and harm us.

The Tail End

Bear with each other and forgive whatever grievances you may have against one another. Forgive as the Lord forgave you.

Colossians 3:13 NIV

217

Endnotes

1. Adapted from the book *Amazing But True Cat Tales*, by Bruce Nash and Allan Zullo, compiled by Muriel MacFarlane. Andrews and McMeel Publishing, Kansas City, MO, 1993. Reprinted by permission of Nash & Zullo Productions, Inc.

2. Reprinted by permission, copyright 1998 by Primedia, Peoria, IL. Courtesy of *Cats Magazine*. Special thanks to Melody Peterson.

3. *Margin*, by Richard A. Swenson, M.D., Used by permission of NavPress/Pinon Press, copyright 1992.

4. Reprinted by permission of HarperCollins Publishers, Inc., excerpt from *Good Time Charlie: A Real Greenwich Village Cat*, by Vivian Cristol, copyright 1965, renewed 1993.

5. Some Titanic facts and references taken from *Titanic: Triumph and Tragedy*, Second Edition, by John P. Eaton and Charles A. Haas, New York, NY; W.W. Norton & Company, 1994. The true name of Jenny's scullion friend is unknown. There was a scullion named William aboard the *Titanic* whose name author Niki Anderson borrowed for this story.

6. *Titanic Survivor: Violet Jessop*, Dobb's Ferry, NY: Sheridan House, 1997, edited by John Maxtone-Graham, 117-18.

7. *The Spokesman-Review*, "The Region," Spokane, WA, February 17, 1997 issue.

8. *277 Secrets Your Cat Wants You to Know*, by Paulette Cooper and Paul Noble, Ten Speed Press, Berkeley, CA, 1997, 232.

9. Adapted from the book *Amazing But True Cat Tales*, by Bruce Nash and Allan Zullo, compiled by Muriel MacFarlane. Andrews and McMeel Publishing, Kansas City, MO, 1993. Reprinted by permission of Nash & Zullo Productions, Inc.

10. Special thanks to the Nelson Branch of the Royal New Zealand Society for the Prevention of Cruelty of Animals, Inc.

11. *Ice Storm '96: Days of Darkness–Days of Cold*, compiled and edited by Shaun O'L. Higgins & Laura B. Lee; a New Media Ventures Book, 1996.

12. Information about the Hofstra cats was supplied by University Archivist, Geri Solomon, Hofstra University, Hempstead, NY, 1998.

Niki and her three cats, Murray, Myles, and Earl

About the Author

Niki says she grew up with a big brother, a dog, a cat, and God. Her mother implanted in her heart the wonder of a loving and all-powerful God so early in life that she does not remember ever being without a sense of His acquaintance. Her mother and father loved cats and agreed that home was not a home unless populated by at least one cat. Thus they had Crummy, Sam, and Walter, among a few.

Within months of Niki's marriage, she and Bob found an abandoned female kitten and named her Margo. Over the next years there was Cynthia Ann, then Thomas, Gary, Thurlough, Dennis, and Wes. And yes, two wonderful children arrived between the additions of the furry friends. Today the Andersons share their home with three tabby brothers, Earl, Murray, and Myles.

Niki enjoys many things besides her cats. She loves family, friends, new words, antiques, prayer retreats, teapots, and flowers. She and her husband of twenty-five years share a deep love for one another and a common love for cats. Their daughter Jodie is in college, majoring in journalism. Their son J. J. is in high school, majoring in studies on the weekdays and snowboarding on the weekends.

Niki loves to create through composing. Her quotation on her author biography best expresses her motivation for everything she writes–"I delight in sharing the truths that have become vital in my own life."

Niki's Inspur-r-ration

Murray seems to be the dominant cat among the three brothers. If, indeed, he is not dominating his siblings, he is dominating the food dish during his few waking hours. His nickname is "Eat-a-Lot." Murray was recently put on a diet to reduce his 21 1/2 pounds to a healthier sum. Thus far, the scales have dropped only 16 ounces. Murray's signature is his habit of crossing his legs. He strikes a pose of great dignity with front paws stretched forward in a casual overlap. Murray favors our nineteen-year-old son, J. J.

Earl is our garrulous guy. He talks enough for all three, earning him the nickname, "Talk-a-Lot." Svelte Earl's general appearance makes him the quintessential cat—trim, long, and busy, also loving, but independent enough to be feline. Earl never misses a chance to swat, in playful gesture, anyone who passes by. Earl is plainly my husband's cat.

$\mathcal{M}$yles is usually addressed as "Myles with a Y." When I assigned him the fine English moniker, I wanted to add the distinguished characteristic of spelling it with a Y (Myles), rather than an I (Miles). I introduced him so many times as "Myles with a Y" that the phrase soon became his name. Myles favors me. Known as "Lounge-a-Lot," his favorite hangout is our bedroom. He loves to lead me to the bed. The moment he is let upstairs in the morning, he runs to our bed, all the while making furtive glances behind him, hoping I am in tow. We lie on the yet unmade bed, I stroke his spine, and tell him how wonderful he is. Then our day begins.

Additional copies of this book,
are available from your local bookstore.

Also by Niki Anderson
What My Cat Has Taught Me About Life

Honor Books
Tulsa, Oklahoma